International and Cultural P

Series editor

Anthony J. Marsella, Professor Emeritus, Univers⸱⸱⸱ ⸱⸱A, USA

Explores problems and challenges to mental health, psychosocial wellbeing, human growth and development, and human welfare that are emerging from our contemporary global context. It advances in psychological knowledge regarding the nature and consequences of the many social, cultural, economic, political, and environmental events and forces that affect individuals and communities throughout the world.

The series covers areas like therapy, assessment, organizational psychology, community psychology, gender, child development, and specific disorders. In addition, it addresses major global challenges such as poverty, peace, urbanization, modernization, refugees, and migration. The series acknowledges the multidisciplinary, multisectoral, and multicultural nature of the global context of our lives, and publishes books that reflect this reality. Publish your next book in this series! Send your manuscript to Series Editor: Anthony J. Marsella, marsella@ hawaii.edu.

More information about this series at http://www.springer.com/series/6089

Patricia Arredondo • Marie L. Miville
Christina M. Capodilupo • Tatiana Vera

Women and the Challenge of STEM Professions

Thriving in a Chilly Climate

 Springer

Patricia Arredondo
Arredondo Advisory Group
Phoenix, AZ, USA

Christina M. Capodilupo
Teachers College
Columbia University
New York, NY, USA

Marie L. Miville
Department of Counseling and
Clinical Psychology
Teachers College
Columbia University
New York, NY, USA

Tatiana Vera
Teachers College
Columbia University
New York, NY, USA

ISSN 1571-5507   ISSN 2197-7984   (electronic)
International and Cultural Psychology
ISBN 978-3-030-62202-2   ISBN 978-3-030-62203-9   (eBook)
https://doi.org/10.1007/978-3-030-62201-5

This Springer imprint is published by the registered company Springer Nature Switzerland AG
The registered company address is: Gewerbestrasse 11, 6330 Cham, Switzerland

For my mom, Beatriz Miville, who always impressed upon me the importance of getting an education and her consistent belief in my abilities and right to be "una doctora."
For my students, past, present, and future

Preface

There are several motivations and reasons for examining the experiences of contemporary women scientists, from their challenges to their ways of thriving, succeeding, and persisting in traditional White male disciplines and academic cultures that remain patriarchal, sexist, and racist. The first relates to my (Arredondo) role as a Co-PI with Dr. Orlando Taylor, an advocate for STEM women leadership. With funding secured by Dr. Taylor from the National Science Foundation, we facilitated an academic leadership program for STEM academic women at Historically Black Colleges and Universities (HBCU) and Tribal Colleges. In my 4 years as an academic coach and faculty member teaching on theories of women's leadership, I learned first-hand about the barriers and sexism faced by African American women, in particular, in male-led departments that are not welcoming to younger women, women who become department chairs, and women who develop collaborations, outside of their departments, just to cite a few examples. Because the goal of the program was to prepare women for academic leadership roles, as a coach I attended to their strengths, support systems, cognitive and emotional approaches to address dilemmas, and specific areas for developing confidence. This was what the women needed and wanted, and they persisted collectively to advance one another [7].

A second motivation came from an article in the Smithsonian magazine that featured Margaret Rossiter, the historian and scientist who dedicated her career to identify women who had been overlooked and marginalized in spite of their scientific successes [6]. This led me to discover historic reasons for women's exclusion, parallels to sociopolitical and sociocultural realities in the USA, and how activism by and for women has slowly changed the landscape for women scientists.

"We are not women in science—we're scientists," proclaimed Donna Strickland upon receiving the Nobel Prize in Physics in 2018. She was the first woman to receive the award in 55 years and only the third in 117 years. Though seemingly astonishing, Dr. Strickland's experience is not unique among women scientists, one of several reasons for our study on women's lived experiences in the challenging world of academia that has historically restricted women from entering, advancing, and enjoying their chosen career in the sciences, engineering, and medicine. This

led to the title of our book: Women and the Challenge of STEM Professions: Thriving in a Chilly Climate.

My colleagues and I are feminists, applying our knowledge and lived experiences as psychologists, and with our graduate student in counseling psychology, to shape the study, we carried out collectively to identify the issues and outcomes that emerged. As we will describe, there has always been a glass ceiling in science and at many levels—in doctoral training, in promotion and tenure cases, with appointments to administrative positions, and with awards and recognition. The perceptions, lived experiences, and viewpoints of women in the sciences derive from multiple contexts and relationships often influenced by conditions and individuals outside of their control. It is our intention to describe historic and contemporary experiences and also hear the voices of contemporary women scientists about their struggles, successes, and recommendations about how to thrive in their chosen professions.

This story is informed by a qualitative study of 10 women scientists, all self-identifying as cisgender women to whom we refer to in this book as "women." The women are from diverse backgrounds in terms of age, ethnicity, race, relationship status, discipline, positions, types of institutions where they studied and are now located, and their varying experiences navigating the academy. Our intent is: (1) to provide psychologists, educators, and employers with real-life narratives of women from culturally diverse backgrounds whose talent is being lost because of unhealthy workplace environments in the STEM fields; (2) to validate women who may think they are alone in workplaces of hostility, marginalization, and invalidation; (3) to report narratives of women who negotiate and achieve success in the midst of hostilities; and (4) to recommend specific practices women can engage and employers can apply to ensure women's safety and career prosperity. There are likely psychologists, like the co-authors, who would be quite interested in this book for both research and practice reasons. It will provide important findings based on first-person narratives as well as critical concerns that women may face as a result of workplace bias/sexism and harassment [12], the "chilly climate" [9], *presumed incompetence* [11], and other dynamics that cause women to question their competence and self-efficacy.

The theoretical framework for this book is feminist psychology influenced by women's intentionality for equity and inclusion in many contexts often through acts of resistance but also with collectivistic acts or changes that will sustain the test of time. The first three chapters provide historic, sociopolitical, and sociocultural context relevant to our study and also perspectives on the continuing challenges facing women scientists. For example, legislation that has affected women's rights in society has also spilled into educational settings, contributing to male-centric attitudes and norms and the glass ceiling, and also opening the door for women to study and eventually join the academy. Dr. Strickland's experience as a Nobel Prize winner in physics after 55 years has precedent. We will discuss the women who were left out of Nobel Prize award ceremonies or whose success was attributed to men. In the case of Marie Curie, the first winner of two Noble prizes, it was her husband who went to Stockholm to receive the award; he was her assistant.

Feminists, feminist psychology, and theories of women's development is discussed in Chap. 2. We were mindful of the Whiteness of these theorists and feminists and included theoretical models and research from women of color. Relevant to our study are concepts of women's ways of knowing [3], in a different voice [8], intersectionality [5], dimensions of personal identity [1, 2], the psychological health of women of color [4], and standpoint theory methodology [10]. Women's leadership is discussed with respect to role congruity theory, women's leadership approaches, and the labyrinths they have to negotiate in universities to claim their position and authority.

Institutional and organizational climate and cultures are essential to appreciate the challenges faced by women scientists. The theoretical models introduced again point to male-centric culture informed by national sociocultural norms and practices, such as hierarchical structures, policies that do not consider women's family responsibilities and challenges for women with disabilities, and the historic academic culture that is slow to flex or change. Mention is made of the current #metoomovemovent, #blacklivesmatter, and COVID-19, all conditions differentially affecting women of color and White women.

In the four Results chapters, based on our thematic analysis, we share themes and women's voices. The themes are: *Support and the Balance Challenge, Healthy Versus Unhealthy Environments, Self-Advocacy, and Awareness and Resistance of Patriarchal/Racist/Oppressive Structural Barriers.* For each theme, there are subthemes with descriptions, for example, of marginalization experiences, mentorship, the "old boy network," and taking a stand versus allowing a man to dictate the rule.

The Discussion chapter brings together the results through a thoughtful and cohesive analysis. We reflect on what we have learned through the voices of the 10 STEM women academics and make connections to other data, sociopolitical realities, and feminist perspectives. Although the women in this study may not describe themselves as feminists or pioneers, their behavior and resolve is similar to that of Matilda Gage, associated with "The Matilda Effect," and Katherine Johnson one the three African American women portrayed in ("Hidden Figures"), women who believe in and value their vocation as scientists and the difference it will make for others.

In our final chapter, we speak directly to academic administrators—deans and department chairs—and offer recommendations for policy changes related to promotion and tenure and work–life balance, structural rearrangements that will benefit women's careers and ways of conducting science, and attention that needs to be given to women's health in unhealthy work environments. To psychologists as well as administrators, we also restate gender biases that adversely affect women's success. These relate to communication style, leadership practices, collectivistic styles of mentorship, and isolation and marginalization because of difference. Generally, clinical psychologists are not prepared in feminist psychology theories, thus they too need to know about contextual conditions that affect women's negative self-attributions that can limit their confidence and careers. We also reflect on the effects of COVID-19 as an opportunity to re-invent academic culture—norms, traditions, ways of leading, and fostering inclusion of women scientists.

Phoenix, AZ, USA   Patricia Arredondo
New York, NY, USA   Marie L. Miville
                                                                Christina M. Capodilupo
                                                                          Tatiana Vera

References

1. Arredondo, P. (1996). *Successful diversity management initiatives: A blueprint for planning and implementation*. Thousand Oaks: SAGE.
2. Arredondo, P., & Glauner, T. (1992). *Personal dimensions of identity model*. Boston: Empowerment Workshops, Inc.
3. Belenky, M. F., Clinchy, B. M., Goldberger, N., & Tarule, J. M. (Eds.). (1986). *Women's ways of knowing: The development of self, voice, and mind* (10th anniversary ed). BasicBooks.
4. Comas-Díaz, L., & Greene, B. (2013). *Psychological health of women of color: Intersections, challenges, and opportunities*. Santa Barbara: Praeger.
5. Crenshaw, K. (n.d.). Demarginalizing the Intersection of Race and Sex: A Black Feminist Critique of Antidiscrimination Doctrine, Feminist Theory and Antiracist Politics. *University of Chicago Legal Forum, 1989*(1), 31.
6. Dominus, S. (2019, October). Women scientists were written out of history. It's Margaret Rossiter's lifelong mission to fix that. *Smithsonian Magazine*. https://www.smithsonianmag.com/science-nature/unheralded-women-scientists-finally-getting-their-due-180973082/
7. Engerman, K., Luster-Teasley, S., Washington, C., & Bolden-Tiller, O. (2016). *Women called to lead: Empowering women of color in academic leadership*. Fielding Graduate University.
8. Gilligan, C. (1982). *In a different voice: Psychological theory and women's development* (Vol. 326). Cambridge, MA: Harvard University Press.
9. Hall, R. M., & Sandler, B. R. (1982). *The classroom climate: A chilly one for women?* https://eric.ed.gov/?id=ED215628
10. Harding, S. G. (1986). *The science question in feminism*. Ithaca: Cornell University Press.
11. Muhs, G. G., Flores Niemann, Y., & González, C. G. (2012). *Presumed incompetent: The intersections of race and class for women in academia* (A. P. Harris, Ed.). University Press of Colorado.
12. National Academies of Sciences, Engineering, and Medicine, Policy and Global Affairs, Committee on Women in Science, Engineering, and Medicine, & Committee on the Impacts of Sexual Harassment in Academia. (2018). *Sexual harassment of women: Climate, culture, and consequences in academic sciences, engineering, and medicine* (F. F. Benya, S. E. Widnall, & P. A. Johnson, Eds.). National Academies Press (US). http://www.ncbi.nlm.nih.gov/books/NBK507206/

Acknowledgments

Patricia Arredondo, Ed.D., NCC

My colleague and friend, Dr. Orlando Taylor is an inspiration and advocate for STEM women through funding that advances their academic leadership careers. I appreciate his steadfast commitment to women's academic success, and to my colleagues and co-authors.

Marie L. Miville, Ph.D.

For my mom, Beatriz Miville, who always impressed upon me the importance of getting an education and her consistent belief in my abilities and right to be "una doctora."

For my students, past, present, and future.

In the words of my mentors:

Dr. Joseph White: Keep the faith!

Dr. Patricia Arredondo: Adelante, siempre adelante/Forward, always forward.

Christina M. Capodilupo, Ph.D.

To my daughter, Madelyn, that she may know a professional life with no limits.

Tatiana Vera, B.A.

To my mother, Mildred Vera, who allowed me to witness resilience and perseverance within academic units from a young age. To my father, Leonardo Vera, who consistently taught me lessons outside of the classroom. To my sister, Katherine Vera, who has shown me what true bravery looks like. To my mentors, Dr. Carolyn Messner, Dr. Angelica Perez-Litwin, Dr. Alain Litwin, and the co-authors of this book. Thank you for your immeasurable guidance.

Contents

**1   The Landscape for Women in the Sciences: Persistence
      Amidst Societal and Institutional Barriers**   1
      No Place for Women Scientists   1
      Women's Rights Legislation in the USA   2
          Legislation Affecting Women in the USA   2
      History of Women in the Sciences   3
          The Matilda Effect   4
          Some Examples of the Matilda Effect and Pioneers
          in the STEM Fields   4
          Shining the Light on Women Scientists   7
      Women's Career Development in STEM and the Male-Centric
      Challenges   8
          Career Development Processes for Women of Color   8
          Career Development for Women in STEM   9
      Professional Associations for Women Scientists   10
      The STEM Pipeline   11
      STEM Academies and Federally Funded Program for Women   13
      Summary   14
      References   14

**2   Feminist Psychology and Sociocultural Precipitants to Women's
      Leadership**   17
      The Emergence of Feminism and Feminist Psychology   17
          First-Wave Feminists   17
          Second-Wave Feminism   18
          Third-Wave Feminists   19
          Black Feminists   20
      Feminist Psychology and the Psychology of Women   21
          Psychology of Women   22
          The Psychology of Women of Color   25
          Standpoint Theory   26

Women's Multiple and Intersecting Identities 27
   Women's Dimensions of Personal, Intersecting Identities 28
   Adverse Identity Self-Perceptions 30
Leadership by Women Through Feminist Perspectives
and Experiences 32
   Emotional Intelligence and Resonant Leadership. 33
Summary. 35
References. 35

**3 Organizational Culture and Climate: Historic Systemic
   Barriers for Women** 41
Introduction. 41
Cultural Variations Across Organizations 42
Situating Women in the Workplace. 43
Women in the World of Work: 2021 44
   2021   Roles and Identity Congruence 45
Academic Culture and Climate. 46
   Concepts and Theories Relevant for Academic Culture 47
The Chilly Climate in Higher Education 48
Organizational Theories and Their Application in Contemporary
Institutions. 49
   Multicultural Organizational Development 50
Sexual Misconduct and Harassment in Higher Education 53
   The Persistence of Sexual Misconduct 54
   Sexual Harassment in the Sciences. 55
   The Double Bind for Women of Color 56
STEM Women in the Academy: Opportunities and the Labyrinth. 57
Diversity, Equity, and Inclusion in the Workplace 57
References. 58

4 Qualitative Methodology: Thematic Analysis 63
Feminist Methodology 63
Procedure 64
Participants 65
Analysis. 65
References. 68

5 "Because You Can't Do It on Your Own": The Role of Support . . . 69
Mentorship 69
Support Outside of Academia. 72
Parenthood Challenge: Support for the Work/Life Balance 73
References. 75

6   **"Providing That Safe Place": Attributes of an Unhealthy**
        vs. Healthy Work Environment 77
        Unhealthy Work Environments............................. 77
        Healthy Environments...................................... 79
        References... 81

7   **"Be Strong!" The Role of Self-Advocacy** 83
        Self-Advocacy as a Personal Quality 83
        Self-Advocacy in Career Decisions 84
        Self-Advocacy in Seeking Support........................... 85

8   **Navigating "Mars": Resisting Structural Barriers in Academia** ... 87
        The Academic Environment as "Old Guard" 87
        Hiring and Tenure Process 90
        The Work of Science....................................... 91

9   **Discussion of Findings** 95
        Limitations 100
        Summary and Conclusions 100
        References... 101

10 **Recommendations and Commitments for Retaining**
        STEM Women in the Academy 103
        Addressing Culture and Climate Issues in the Academy 103
            Policies for Hiring and Promotion and Tenure 105
            Recommendations from Participants 107
            Health and Mental Health in the Academy.................. 109
            STEM Diversity Initiatives and Resources.................. 109
        Recommendations for Psychologists 110
            Closing Thoughts 112
        References... 112

Index... 115

About the Authors

Patricia Arredondo, Ed.D., NCC, has dedicated her extensive career to addressing social justice issues on behalf of marginalized groups. This manifests in her scholarship, servant leadership, and mentorship. She is a recognized scholar in the areas of cultural competency development, women's leadership, immigrant mental health, and Latinx higher education and mental health. As a result of her organizational consulting, she has distinguished herself in the field of strategic diversity initiatives. She attributes her zeal for advocacy to her father whom she describes as a feminist. With her mother and Abuela, she had role models of strength and courage. Patricia is the founding president of the National Latinx Psychological Association, past president of the American Counseling Association, past chair of the board of directors of the American Association of Hispanics in Higher Education, and a fellow of the American Psychological Association. She is a licensed psychologist and president of the Arredondo Advisory Group.

Marie L. Miville, Ph.D., is professor of psychology and education and vice dean for Faculty Affairs at Teachers College, Columbia University. She is the author of 2 books and over 65 publications dealing with multicultural issues in counseling and psychology. Dr. Miville is an associate editor of the *Journal of Multicultural Counseling and Development* and is serving or has served on several other editorial boards. She is the past president of the National Latinx Psychological Association (NLPA), the book series editor for the American Psychological Association (APA) Division 44, and previously served as vice president for education and training for the APA Division 17. Dr. Miville is an APA fellow (Division 17 and 45). Prior to her appointment as vice dean, Dr. Miville served as the college ombudsperson, program director for the master's course in counseling, doctoral director of training of counseling psychology, and the chair of the Department of Counseling and Clinical Psychology.

Christina M. Capodilupo, Ph.D., is adjunct professor in the Department of Counseling and Clinical Psychology at Teachers College, Columbia University. She has a master's degree in education, specializing in gender studies from Harvard's Graduate School of Education. Christina has spent her academic career studying how experiences of social class, race, and gender influence and impact a person's developing sense of self and well-being. She has extensively researched how experiences of discrimination manifest for marginalized groups, and more specifically how subtle acts of racism, classism, and sexism shape a person's psyche. She has authored journal articles, book chapters, and books on the topic of racial and gender microaggressions. Christina's clinical and research interests also focus on body image and eating disorders; she has published extensively on how these issues manifest for women of color. She has four young children at home and has experienced the motherhood balance challenge first hand!

Tatiana Vera, B.A., is a doctoral student in the Department of Counseling and Clinical Psychology at Teachers College, Columbia University. She has a B.A. degree in psychology with a minor in Spanish literature and cultures from Barnard College and was an Athena Leadership Scholar/Collegiate Science and Technology Entry Program Scholar. Although young, she has a long history of bolstering spaces for women and Latinx communities. Upon graduation, she served as student relations co-chair for the Latino Alumni Association of Columbia University. Tatiana has authored and conducted research on topics ranging from the concept of self-esteem in adolescent women in the USA and Ecuador, managing cancer in the workplace, and has co-created workshops with mentors for adolescent Latinas to implement what she has learned. She hopes to continue her advocacy in and out of academic settings in the years ahead and that her dissertation will coalesce her interests.

Chapter 1
The Landscape for Women in the Sciences: Persistence Amidst Societal and Institutional Barriers

No Place for Women Scientists

As a doctoral student at Yale, Margaret Rossiter attended weekly informal gatherings of professors and students from her science department. The lack of women in the sciences had not escaped her, so she innocently asked the question one afternoon: "Were there ever women scientists?" The firm response was "never" and "none." It was 1969, and long before then, Marie Curie had earned two Nobel Prizes, one for physics and the other for chemistry. She was the first person ever to win two Nobel Prizes. Thus the answer "none" was not accurate. Margaret's professors, however, suggested that Marie Curie was merely her husband's helper. History will also attest that though Curie was named the Nobel Prize recipient, it was her husband who attended the award ceremony.

The film "Hidden Figures" illustrated the assumptions and conscious biases about women of color scientists considered incapable of doing mathematical analyses. The White male scientists did not hold back their dismissive attitudes even when the women demonstrated their intelligence and skill. Women in STEM professions, long considered a male bastion, continue to break through systemic barriers slowly, but whether in industry or the academy, women scientists are still outliers. In an interview, Rossiter stated, "As scientists they {women} were atypical women; as women, they were unusual scientists" [7].

As we sought to identify early women scientists for this chapter, we relied heavily on two of Rossiter's books, *Women Scientists in America: Struggles and Strategies to 1940* and *Women Scientists in America: Before Affirmative Action, 1940–1972*. These provide the most accurate and comprehensive sources of women scientists through 1972. Again from Rossiter, we learned of *American Men and Women in Science*, formerly *Men in Science*, a directory of select scientists and their contributions.

P. Arredondo et al., *Women and the Challenge of STEM Professions*, International and Cultural Psychology, https://doi.org/10.1007/978-3-030-62201-5_1

Multiple examples illustrate the context in the USA that has historically perpetuated the marginalization of women in general in society, education, academia, leadership roles, and, of course, STEM. In the next section, we will describe an historical and sociopolitical chronology of women's rights legislation that is meant to frame the realities for women's access and exclusion in different institutions, such as higher education. Women scientists in the USA were often overlooked because they were women, women of color, and younger women, seemingly a threat to male scientists.

Women's Rights Legislation in the USA

A timeline on women's rights in the USA demonstrates the intentional exclusion of rights and access given to men and other choices specific to women's sex [16]. In short, there have been systematic legislative practices that have had subsequent influences on women as students in higher education, as scientists, in the workplace, and in visible roles of authority. A few examples will be highlighted.

Legislation Affecting Women in the USA

- 1769: The country's settlement included the adoption of the English system, deeming that women could not own property or keep their earnings.
- 1777: All states at the time passed laws taking away women's right to vote. This coincided with the signing of the Declaration of Independence, referring to "free men" and excluding persons of African and American Indian heritage.
- 1848: 300 women and men signed the Declaration of Sentiments at the Women's Rights Convention in Seneca Falls, NY. The Declaration was to end discrimination against women. A leader at the conference on behalf of African American women was Harriet Tubman, an abolitionist and social justice crusader.
- 1890: Wyoming became the first state to grant women the right to vote.
- 1920: the 19th amendment is passed, giving women the right to vote in the USA. This occurred merely 100 years ago.
- 1923: The first version of the Equal Rights Amendment was introduced, specifying that both men and women would have equal rights throughout the USA.
- 1953: For the first time, a woman was approved to undergo astronaut testing. In 1963, NASA canceled the women's space program. Twenty years later, in 1983, the first woman was sent into space.
- 1963: The Equal Pay Act is passed by Congress, declaring equal pay regardless of sex, color, religion, national origin, and race.
- 1964: The Civil Rights Act prohibits sex discrimination.

- 1968: President Lyndon B. Johnson signed an executive order "prohibiting sex discrimination by government contractors" and mandating affirmative action plans for hiring women.
- 1972: The Equal Employment Opportunity Act was signed into law and established the EEO Commission to address employment discrimination based on sex, race, color, national origin, disability, political beliefs, and marital or familial status.
- 1972: Title IX was part of the Education Amendment of 1972 and written to prohibit discrimination in education programs receiving federal support. It reads: "No person in the United States shall, based on sex, be excluded from participation in, be denied the benefits of, or be subjected to discrimination under any education program or activity receiving Federal financial assistance." The law provides equal rights in sports for women and men and is invoked in sexual harassment and assault cases. The champion and "godmother" of Title IX is Bernice Sandler (1928–2020), a woman's activist and psychologist who led studies to identify behaviors that affected women and men differently in classrooms.
- 1974: Based on a Supreme Court ruling, "It is illegal to force pregnant women to take maternity leave based on the assumption that they are incapable" of fulfilling their job responsibilities because of their physical condition.
- 1982: The Equal Rights Amendment does not have sufficient votes to be ratified.
- 1986: The Supreme Court ruled that a hostile work environment could be invoked in sexual harassment cases.
- 1992: Declaration of the Year of the Woman following Anita Hill's testimony of sexual harassment against Justice Clarence Thomas.
- January 15, 2020: Virginia becomes the 38th state to ratify the Equal Rights Amendment.

It is noteworthy that, to date, the USA does not have an Equal Rights Amendment, and unlike other democracies, the country has never had a woman president. Though there is an increasing presence of women elected to federal and state legislatures, the voting electorate still favors male candidates. 2016 was an unusual year with a diversity of women elected to the House of Representatives and returning Nancy Pelosi to leadership as Speaker of the House. The 2020 election may introduce more women into visible leadership roles.

History of Women in the Sciences

Bringing the history of women scientists to the forefront became the lifework of Margaret Rossiter, Marie Underhill Noll Professor of the History of Science, Cornell University. She researched and authored groundbreaking literature on women scientists whose identities and accomplishments were buried in archives, particularly at women's institutions. Her initial studies, *Women Scientists in America: Before Affirmative Action, 1940–1972* [26] and *Women Scientists in America—Struggles and Strategies* (1982), identified hundreds of women scientists beginning with Maria Mitchell (1818–1889), an astronomer who discovered a comet named "Miss Mitchell's Comet" in 1847. Mitchell was a women's rights activist and a founding member of the Association for the Advancement of Women in 1873 and the first woman elected Fellow of the American Academy of Arts and Sciences in 1948 [15].

Through her research, Rossiter identified several themes as these relate to the exclusion of women scientists. These included "territorial segregation." Women were found primarily in women's colleges and "hierarchical segregation" because women were generally in junior professor positions. The theme of "restrictive logic" also emerged in her research. She identified two phrases commonly used by men as examples of restrictive logic as they argued against promotion and tenure for women. These were *there was no precedent* and they were *unprepared*. The mindsets against change and inclusion and the superior patriarchal attitudes toward women were pervasive and overt.

The Matilda Effect

In 1993, Rossiter coined the phrase "the Matilda effect" about women who did not receive credit for their scientific inventions [25]. The origin of the term was Matilda Gage, a suffragist, abolitionist, and Native American rights activist whose work was denied credit when she left the mainstream, conservative women's movement to form a radical suffrage organization. Ironically, it was suffragists Susan B. Anthony and Elizabeth Cady Stanton with whom she had collaborated, who purged any references to her in their books *History of Woman Suffrage*. Gage was born in a home in Cicero, New York in 1826 that was a site for the Underground Railroad. Her early education taught by her father included Greek, physiology, and mathematics, and she authored *Woman as Inventor* (1883) and *Women's Rights Catechism* in 1871 [32].

Some Examples of the Matilda Effect and Pioneers in the STEM Fields

Rossiter found many examples of women excluded from recognition for their contribution to scientific discoveries. Unless contemporary STEM women were to have a course about women scientists, they might not know of these women. Still, Rossiter identified them in her first volume of *Women Scientists in America* [24]. A few of these women and their accomplishments are cited here:

- Jocelyn Bell Burnell (1943–) was a doctoral student in radio astronomy from Belfast, Northern Ireland, at Cambridge University in the late 1960s. When her team won the Nobel Prize in 1974, only the men were included in the citation. Finally, 44 years later, Burnell was recognized as the person who discovered an astronomical object that led to the identification of pulsars.
- Chen-Shiung Wu (1912–1977) emigrated from China in the 1930s and was recruited to work on the Manhattan Project. An experimental physicist, she worked on uranium enrichment. As a result of her work, two male colleagues were awarded the Nobel Prize in Physics in 1957; she did not share in the award. She was the first woman president of the American Physical Society.
- Klara Dan Von Neumann (1911–1963) was a self-taught mathematician. She was the primary developer of a computer coding program in the 1940s. When a paper was published regarding the work, her name was not included.
- Frances Oldham Kelsey (1914–2015), a pharmacist and physician with the FDA, was pressured to approve the thalidomide drug. She protested because of inadequate tests to support the use of the drug, thereby sparing thousands of infants who otherwise would have been born with deformities. The drug had already been approved in 46 other countries.
- Roger Arliner Young (1889–1964) was the first African American to earn a doctorate in zoology, graduating from Howard University. Her specialty fields were biology, marine biology, and zoology. She conducted her research on the "anatomy of paramecium and the effects of radiation on sea urchin eggs" at the Center for Marine Biology, Woods Hole, MA. Young faced many obstacles as a woman of color, breaking barriers that others would follow. She also cared for her mother, an invalid and homebound, who added responsibilities to her highly demanding professional life.
- Barbara McClintock (1902–1992) was the first woman to receive a Nobel Prize in Physiology or Medicine that was not shared. She was a cytogeneticist who studied the mobility of genes on chromosomes.
- Grace Murray Hopper (1906–1992) was a rear admiral in the US Navy, a mathematician, and a computer scientist. She was on a team that created "the first computer language" program that translated English into computer code language.
- Bertha Parker Pallan Cody (1907–1978) of Seneca and Abenaki heritage is known as the first Native American woman archeologist. She uncovered "Scorpion Hill" during an expedition that led to an exhibition at the Southwest Museum of Los Angeles where she later became the director.
- Marie Maynard Daly (1921–2003) was the first African American woman to earn a Ph.D. in Chemistry from Columbia University in 1947. In her research, she identified links between cholesterol and heart disease and the effects of smoking on the lungs.

Hidden Figures: African American Women Scientists

The film *Hidden Figures* brought to visibility three African American women scientists at NASA, overlooked and marginalized. However, their knowledge was essential in the space race era with the Soviet Union and John Glenn's spacewalk. The space race was also occurring during the civil rights movement. Katherine Johnson (1918–2020), a mathematician, Dorothy Vaughan (1910–2008), a mathematician; and Mary Jackson (1921–2005), an engineer, were known as human computers, but they faced dual obstacles because of gender and race. Before joining NASA, Vaughan had worked at the Langley Memorial Aeronautical Laboratory beginning in 1943. However, she worked with other African Americans separately from their White colleagues. Jackson was known for her expertise with wind tunnels and flight experiments; her task was to extract relevant data from flights. Johnson applied her talents to many of the space shuttle plans and implementations. She was known for her accuracy with computations and other essential calculations. It was reported that John Glenn trusted Johnson's mathematical calculations more than machines, thus attributing "human computers" to the women [13].

Identifying Latina Scientists: Even More Hidden

Identifying Latina scientists born and educated in the USA with notable prominence and visibility was a more significant challenge. There are renowned scientists from Latin America who have been awarded for their scientific accomplishments but not the case for Latinas in the states. However, with a little investigation, a few women were identified:

- Antonia Novello (1944–) from Fajardo, Puerto Rico, a physician and public health administrator, served as the 14th Surgeon General from 1990 to 1993. She was the first woman and first Latina to serve in this capacity. Before that, she was Deputy Director of the National Institute of Child Health and Human Development [6].
- France A. Cordova (1947–) is an astrophysicist and held many senior administrative roles during her distinguished career. She was the youngest person, the first woman, and the first Latina to serve as NASA's chief scientist. She was also the 14th Director of the National Science Foundation, serving from 2013 to 2016. Dr. Cordova is president emerita of the University of California, Riverside, and Purdue University. She is a Fellow of the American Association for the Advancement of Science and the Association for Women in Science, among other prestigious associations [18].
- Lydia Villa Komaroff (1947–) was the third Mexican American woman in the USA to earn a doctorate in the sciences (a molecular and cellular biologist) in 1975 (finding the first two women fell short). As an undergraduate, she was told by her advisor that "women do not belong in chemistry" and therefore switched majors to biology. She was involved in groundbreaking research, contributing to

the discovery that a molecule known to be associated with Alzheimer's disease (amyloid-beta) causes degeneration of brain cells (neurons), work done in conjunction with a postdoctoral fellow in her laboratory. As a graduate student at MIT, she was a co-founding member of the Society for the Advancement of Chicanos/Hispanics and Native Americans in Science (SACNAS) [33].

- Ellen Ochoa (1958–) of Mexican American heritage is the first Latina selected to be an astronaut and the first in space on the Space Shuttle Discovery. An engineer, she has been on four missions and is the first Latina and the second woman to become Director of NASA's Lyndon B. Johnson Space Center in Houston [23].

Shining the Light on Women Scientists

American Men in Science was first published in 1906 (Cattell) and in 1971 was broadened to include women. It is now titled *American Men and Women of Science, Physical and Biological Sciences*, with its 34th edition published in 2016. It is a biographical compilation of scientists in the physical and natural sciences from the USA and Canada. Inclusion is based on the merit of publications in esteemed journals, distinguished training, positions, and achievements and requires a nomination process. Scientists not from the USA or Canada are included if most of their work was done in North America.

During her fellowship at Harvard in the early 1970s, Rossiter found *American Men in Science*, and much to her surprise, she came across entries about women scientists. These included botanists and geologists, and she discovered connections among them; they seemed to have professional relationships. This discovery was the initiation and affirmation of her exploratory process about the existence of women scientists and their contributions.

To shine a light on the absence of women scientists in public spaces, Anne Fausto-Sterling, a professor of biology and gender studies at Brown University, and her former student, Maria Weinstock, launched Wikipedia edit-thons. Their purpose was to provide entries about women scientists and their achievements through this online directory. During her Wikipedia edit-thons, Fausto-Sterling, a fellow of the American Association for the Advancement of Science, found a minuscule entry about Rossiter much to her surprise. This entry led her to provide a more comprehensive listing about Rossiter in her women and science online directory [20].

The Lancet, a prestigious medical journal, had an entire issue addressing the underrepresentation of women in science, reporting that less than 30% of women were researchers in science [7]. There are multiple reasons for underrepresentation as has been reviewed thus far, but ignoring women's presence is a loss for the field of science and women considering a career in STEM.

This first section was designed to provide context to the oversight and neglect of women male scientists and the concerted efforts of other women scientists and advocates of women to recognize their existence and contributions. Though progress has been made and there are more women in the STEM fields, there is a continuing need to provide mentorship, support, and professional networks to thrive. All of this falls into a discussion of STEM women's career development in subsequent sections of this chapter.

Women's Career Development in STEM and the Male-Centric Challenges

Vocational psychology and theories of career development have been developed primarily and historically by White men and taught through the present, to master's and doctoral students in counseling and applied psychology programs without consideration of how these applied or did not apply to women, ethnic-racial minority groups, to individuals of other diverse identities, and in international settings. The main focus of vocational psychology has been on assessing career interests and career choices, looking at work-life balance, and wellness in the workplace. Research from career interest inventories [11, 12] and the lifespan career development theory of Super [30] was based primarily on White, upper-middle-class boys and men, often drawn from samples of convenience. Thus, norms have not considered other populations, including women, and the gender bias inherent in the assessment norms.

Applying gender role stereotypes to justify men's dominance in male occupations and feminine qualities for women's occupations has been long-standing. Cejka and Eagly [5] examined attributes for occupational success that research participants applied to 80 occupations. These attributes were masculine physical, feminine physical masculine personality, feminine personality, masculine cognitive, and feminine cognitive. For female-dominated professions, it was assumed that feminine personality or physical attributes were requisites for success. As with male occupations, there were similar findings. Participants attributed masculine personality or physical characteristics as more essential for male occupations. Stereotypes influenced the justification of gender hierarchy; occupations perceived to require masculine personality and masculine cognitive attributes for success also related to higher-earning professions. The sciences, engineering, and medicine have been considered masculine fields for many years. The persistence of such stereotypes can adversely affect women seeking to enter these fields and the environments for evolving their careers.

Career Development Processes for Women of Color

Career development for women of color merits attention because of the shortcomings in quality research findings for theory development in mainstream counseling and psychology literature. There are times when research that is grounded in critical race theory inherently sustains support for research findings in outcomes of women of color as opposed to White women. Therefore, it is arguably analyzed through the lens of competitiveness between majority and minority women, missing the importance of collaboration as advocated in feminist identity development, which serves importance in successfully navigating a male-dominated field for both White women and women of color. Research that focuses only on the career development of African American women, it is reported, excludes the vast diversity of other groups of ethnically and racial minority women. However, all ethnic and racial minority women have their own unique experiences, and their career development processes need to be examined through the ethnic and racial womanist lens. Women of color hold a position of at least a dual-status minority, being both women and of color. The identities speak to critical intersections for STEM women of color in a male-dominated workplace, and the role is characteristically marginalized. Marginalization presents a barrier to success. An ecological theory developed by Cook et al. [35] has given a takeaway that women of color's successful career development examines the importance of interactions between the woman and the environment.

Career Development for Women in STEM

Inequities in terms of access and opportunities, gender discrimination, and sexual harassment in graduate school and the academy, and recognition and support are structural and interpersonal factors that have affected women in STEM personally and professionally. Findings from a consensus study by the National Academies of Sciences, Engineering, and Medicine [17] illustrate the multiple barriers women encounter on their way to becoming a scientist, engineer, or physician, due to sexual harassment, climate, and culture.

Attention to career development for women in STEM is under-researched more so than career development for women in general, and identity groups of ethnic and racial minority women, and women across the lifespan. Factors informing career development specifically for women in STEM were identified in three categories: level of women's attitudes, interactions between women as individuals and society, and societal influences [9]. *Individual attitudes* relate to abilities, women's interests, and self-efficacy with vocational interests and self-efficacy being salient influences on women's attitudes toward their work. Belief in one's ability to accomplish a task and trust in a positive outcome is known as self-efficacy. *Interactions between women as individuals and society* point to individual and social factors, or, better said, identity factors such as sexual orientation, and how these interplay with one's career development process. *Societal influences* specific to women's career development include gender-bound socialization processes, societal factors that affect opportunities for women's career choices, and economic factors influencing the labor market that may see a need for women in the STEM sectors or, conversely, women as a barrier to men seeking to be in STEM fields.

Social Cognitive Career Theory

Another perspective on STEM women's career development was explained through the interrelatedness of career development and interest development specific to how choices are made and how success is obtained as related to academic and career pursuits [14]. Social cognitive career theory (SCCT), as it was called, was based on Albert Bandura's theory of social cognitive development [4], addressing behaviors that are learned and motivated. SCCT is built around three variables: self-efficacy beliefs, outcome expectations, and goals. The theory's construction grew out of the intention to understand the underrepresentation of women in math and science careers [9]. In theory, persistent interest in an activity is mediated by a personal view of competence and an expectation that valued outcomes will result. As will be discussed in the next section, the persistence of women in STEM careers also requires supportive structures that affirm their competence and contributions.

Professional Associations for Women Scientists

Women-centered professional associations can be found for almost all disciplines today. Quite often, women have created spaces to enrich their experiences for mentorship and colleagueship. In male-founded associations, the same opportunities to thrive and to be recognized do not exist. Women in the sciences may be found in mainstream associations and specifically ones designated for women. The significant associations in the USA are highlighted:

- The National Academy of Sciences (NAS), also known as the National Academy, was established in 1863 to recognize scientists in various STEM disciplines. The National Academy of Engineering was established in 1964 and the National Academy of Medicine in 1974 under the charter of the NAS. Individuals may be nominated and elected as Fellows to the National Academy of Medicine, Engineering, or Science. In 1989, there were 1516 members among these 57 women. It was reported then that women were being admitted at a "dismal rate." In 2016, there were 2350 members and 450 foreign associates [28].
  The National Academies of Sciences includes the disciplines of Physical and Mathematical Sciences, Biological Sciences, Engineering and Applied Sciences, Biomedical Sciences, Behavioral and Social Sciences, and Applied Biological, Agricultural, and Environmental Sciences. The website for the National Academies of Sciences profiles the presidents of the Academy from 1863 to 2016; all are White men. According to the site, Marcia McNutt is the current president with her term expiring in 2022 [29]. Her picture is not included on the website page with that of other presidents but appears elsewhere. The governing board of NAS is inclusive of gender but has only one male African American pictured on the listing [29].
- The Society of Women Engineers (SWE) was founded in 1950. Its mission is to be the world's most massive advocate for women in engineering, technology, and a catalyst for change [1]. SWE welcomes students and professionals alike.

- The Association for Women in Science (AWIS) was established in 1971 and positions itself as an advocacy organization for women in STEM professions. Their mission is to drive excellence and achieve equity and full participation for women in all work contexts [3]. Among its coalition partners are the Society of Hispanic Professional Engineers, the American Association of University Women, and the Society of Women Engineers. In 1975, AWIS and the NAACP won a lawsuit against the Office of Civil Rights (OCR) for discrimination in higher education based on sex and race.
- STEM Women of Color Conclave (SWOCC) serves women of color in higher education on a national scale. Established in 2010, it hosts an annual conference and leadership institute. The SWOCC mission is to support women in their personal and professional development and career advancement [31].

The STEM Pipeline

The areas of study within the STEM field are varied—from agricultural sciences to engineering, to medicine, to computer technology. In 2017, there was almost an equal number of men and women in STEM doctoral programs. However, the differences concerning engineering and the health and medical sciences are noteworthy.

	Men	Women
Biological and agricultural sciences	442,477	50,965
Engineering	119,770	40,370
Health and medical sciences	53,147	186,889
Mathematics and computer sciences	77,555	36,590
Physical and earth sciences	33,897	20,352
Totals	726,776	335,166

Okahana and Zhou [19], Table C.21

Doctoral degrees granted by the fields also vary. Data for 2017–2018 is presented below.

	Total	Men	Women
Biological and agricultural sciences	8543	4014	4439
Engineering	9981	7507	2474
Health sciences	15,402	4466	10,936
Mathematical and computer sciences	3437	2570	867
Physical and earth sciences	5144	3082	2062

Okahana and Zhou [19], Table B.25

Concerning ethnicity and race, including US citizens and permanent residents only, CGS reports on enrollment between 2008 and 2018 for each ethnic and racial group. The numbers are small for the four underrepresented groups. For example, from Table C-20, *NCSES of the National Science Foundation has info on doctoral grads by sex, ethnicity, and race but not disaggregated sufficiently.*

Table C.20: Total Graduate Enrollment by Broad Field and Race/Ethnicity, 2008 to 2018 (U.S. Citizens and Permanent Residents Only)

Broad Field	American Indian/Alaska Native			Asian/Pacific Islander *			Black/African American		
	% Change, '17–'18	Avg. Annual % Change, '13–'18	Avg. Annual % Change, '08–'18	% Change, '17–'18	Avg. Annual % Change, '13–'18	Avg. Annual % Change, '08–'18	% Change, '17–'18	Avg. Annual % Change, '13–'18	Avg. Annual % Change, '08–'18
Total	1.2%	-2.2%	-3.0%	8.1%	3.8%	3.0%	1.1%	0.5%	0.4%
Arts & Humanities	-8.4%	-5.3%	-4.9%	-0.3%	-3.0%	-1.0%	-2.5%	0.2%	-0.3%
Bio. & Agric. Sci.	-1.1%	-0.6%	-2.7%	4.9%	5.0%	3.8%	3.0%	4.4%	3.6%
Business	15.0%	-0.4%	-2.2%	5.1%	3.8%	1.7%	0.8%	5.3%	4.1%
Education	1.8%	-2.7%	-4.2%	3.8%	1.8%	1.1%	1.0%	-0.1%	-1.0%
Engineering	1.7%	-0.3%	-3.3%	2.7%	1.4%	1.5%	-0.4%	0.5%	1.2%
Health Sciences	-0.9%	-0.2%	1.2%	3.0%	6.2%	9.7%	4.5%	4.8%	8.7%
Math & Comp. Sci.	6.1%	-0.2%	-2.5%	17.6%	19.0%	12.5%	8.7%	8.8%	8.3%
Physical & Earth Sci.	-12.1%	-4.1%	-4.0%	3.1%	3.0%	3.2%	2.0%	0.7%	0.1%
Public Admin. & Svcs.	-1.7%	-0.5%	-0.9%	2.3%	1.9%	1.7%	0.0%	2.0%	1.9%
Social & Behav. Sci.	-4.1%	-5.0%	-3.9%	5.2%	0.4%	0.4%	0.6%	0.5%	0.6%
Other Fields	9.6%	9.0%	-2.8%	5.9%	2.8%	0.6%	-0.5%	2.3%	1.6%

Broad Field	Hispanic/Latino			White		
	% Change, '17–'18	Avg. Annual % Change, '13–'18	Avg. Annual % Change, '08–'18	% Change, '17–'18	Avg. Annual % Change, '13–'18	Avg. Annual % Change, '08–'18
Total	7.3%	6.1%	6.6%	1.2%	-0.4%	-0.3%
Arts & Humanities	0.2%	1.3%	2.7%	-3.5%	-4.1%	-2.7%
Bio. & Agric. Sci.	10.6%	10.5%	13.0%	1.7%	0.6%	1.4%
Business	10.4%	8.6%	8.9%	3.5%	2.2%	1.0%
Education	3.9%	4.6%	3.4%	0.0%	-1.1%	-2.2%
Engineering	6.7%	5.3%	9.4%	0.7%	-0.2%	1.2%
Health Sciences	6.9%	12.8%	20.2%	1.9%	2.3%	5.3%
Math & Comp. Sci.	15.9%	13.0%	14.7%	7.5%	5.0%	4.0%
Physical & Earth Sci.	7.5%	9.9%	10.1%	-0.3%	-0.4%	0.6%
Public Admin. & Svcs.	6.4%	7.6%	11.5%	-0.1%	-0.2%	1.1%
Social & Behav. Sci.	5.5%	2.7%	4.1%	-1.1%	-2.5%	-1.2%
Other Fields	7.4%	9.4%	7.9%	0.6%	-1.1%	-2.5%

* Includes Asians and Native Hawaiians/Other Pacific Islanders
Notes: See Appendix D for the survey taxonomy. See page 20 for a description of each race/ethnicity category.
Source: CGS/GRE Survey of Graduate Enrollment and Degrees

Okahana and Zhou [19], Table C.20

Per the Society of Women Engineers, the number of women in engineering in the USA has not increased since the early 2000s with implications for women in the profession [22]). In 2017–2018, 33.9% of women were full professors compared with 51.4% of men [27]. Only 17.4% of tenure/tenure-track faculty are women [27]. Women are most represented in the life sciences-related discipline with one out of four tenure/tenure-track faculty. Conversely, the lowest numbers for women are in the aerospace engineering fielding with less than 12% [27].

Among doctoral-level scientists and engineers in universities and 4-year colleges, women are underrepresented at various positions and levels. In 2017, women represented about 35% of deans, department heads, and chairs in these institutions. Similarly, they represented about 36% of the research faculty and teaching faculty. Overall, they had slightly higher representation in the academic positions of adjunct faculty (41.2%) and postdoctoral researchers (40.5%) [34].

Among all science, engineering, and health doctoral degree holders employed in universities and 4-year colleges, women represent less than half of the faculty across all ranks. In engineering, women represent about 15% of the total faculty and less than 10% of full professors. Among engineering faculty, women of color represent less than 3% of full professors, about 6% of associate professors, and less than 9% of assistant professors. The doctoral student enrollment data and earned degree data are not disaggregated by gender and race and ethnicity, so it is hard to know if ethnic minority individuals have increased their participation rates [34].

The persistence of women in STEM professions is a continuing source of concern for researchers, leaders in the academy, and professional societies. In a 2013 report [21], five reasons were cited for the gap between men and women in STEM careers, particularly in the academy. At the top of the list were women's continuing conflicts with their career and childcare responsibilities. It was noted that there is a long trajectory from graduate school to postdoctoral appointments and then on to a tenure-track university position. This means that women are later in their late 20s and 30s when the priority for having children may become heightened. Though men may follow the same career trajectory, they generally do not have to think about childbearing and managing their home and work life. As a result, it was pointed out that women drop out of their careers more than men after receiving their Ph.D. Second is the pervasive issue of bias, formal, and unconscious. The report noted that scientific terms are often associated with male terms versus female terms. If presented with the words astrophysics and engineering on a free association checklist, men would be associated with these terms, not women. The biases in the professionals are one of many reasons professional associations and federal programs have actively engaged in supporting women in STEM.

STEM Academies and Federally Funded Program for Women

The historical exclusion of women from the sciences, the continuing systemic barriers to enrollment and support, and other societal obstacles have led to the creation of programs for STEM women across the country. Many institutions receive support from the National Science Foundation's Broadening Participation/Diversity Office, designed to provide resources for underrepresented groups and diverse institutions, i.e., Historically Black Colleges and Universities [10]. Other examples from the Broadening Participation program include ELATES, a STEM academic leadership program hosted by Drexel University involving women in projects that support their professional development and advancement [8]. The Outstanding Underrepresented Research Scientists (OURS) program has had four cohorts (N = 64) of women academics from Historically Black Colleges and Universities and Tribal Colleges (Personal communication). Hosted by two professional schools of psychology in collaboration with NSF, the program supported the advancement of academic women in leadership roles at their respective institutions. Lastly, the National Science Foundation's ADVANCE program aims to increase the representation and promotion of women in academic science and engineering careers [2]. Since 2001, the NSF has invested over $270M to support ADVANCE projects at more than 100 institutions of higher education and STEM-related not-for-profit organizations in 41 states, the District of Columbia, and Puerto Rico, including 24 EPSCoR jurisdictions [2].

Summary

Historical accounts of the absence of women in the sciences and the barriers they faced began to put into perspective the status of women in the sciences today. In this initial opening chapter, it seemed necessary to provide an accounting of women's rights legislation to combat exclusionary and discriminatory practices that prevented women access to educational opportunities and careers. Although a listing of some women scientists is provided, it was a challenge to find these lists, particularly for women of color. Often, women scientists had to forge their pathways alone or collectively and give one another voice through scholarship, associations, and formal recognition. Many singular women became engineers, astronauts, and biologists, but they were considered trailblazers, not typical scientists. The STEM pipeline for women is increasing through systematic programs for girls, college, and doctoral students, but the retention of women in the science professions is challenging. Fortunately, federally funded programs and professional societies provide some of the necessary structures and resources to ensure access and the success of STEM women in the academy.

References

1. *About SWE.* (n.d.). Society of women engineers. Retrieved May 16, 2020, from https://swe.org/about-swe/
2. *ADVANCE at a Glance | NSF – National Science Foundation.* (n.d.). Retrieved May 18, 2020, from https://www.nsf.gov/crssprgm/advance/
3. *AWIS History.* (2016, June 23). Association for women in science. https://www.awis.org/about-awis/awis-history/
4. Bandura, A. (1975). Analysis of modeling processes. *School Psychology Review, 4*(1), 4–10. https://doi.org/10.1080/02796015.1975.12086341.

5. Cejka, M. A., & Eagly, A. H. (1999). Gender-stereotypic images of occupations correspond to the sex segregation of employment—Mary Ann Cejka, Alice H. Eagly, 1999. *Personality and Social Psychology Bulletin, 25*(4), 413–423.

6. *Changing the Face of Medicine | Antonia Novello*. (2003, October 14). Changing the face of medicine. https://cfmedicine.nlm.nih.gov/physicians/biography_239.html

7. Dominus, S. (2019, October). Women scientists were written out of history. It's Margaret Rossiter's lifelong mission to fix that. *Smithsonian Magazine*. https://www.smithsonianmag.com/science-nature/unheralded-women-scientists-finally-getting-their-due-180973082/

8. *ELATES at Drexel®*. (2020, January 7). Office of the Provost. https://drexel.edu/provost/initiatives/elates/

9. Fouad, N. A., & Ihle, K. (2017). Effective strategies for career counseling with women. In *Handbook of counseling women* (2nd ed., pp. 317–339). Thousand Oaks: Sage Publications, Inc.

10. *Historically Black Colleges and Universities—Undergraduate Program | NSF – National Science Foundation*. (n.d.). Retrieved May 18, 2020, from https://www.nsf.gov/funding/pgm_summ.jsp?pims_id=5481

11. Holland, J. L. (1973). *Making vocational choices: A theory of careers*. Prentice-Hall.

12. Holland, J. L. (1997). *Making vocational choices: A theory of vocational personalities and work environments* (3rd ed., pp. xiv, 303). Psychological Assessment Resources.

13. Howell, E. (2020, February 24). *NASA's Real "Hidden Figures."* Space.Com. https://www.space.com/35430-real-hidden-figures.html

14. Lent, R. W., Brown, S. D., & Hackett, G. (2002). Social cognitive career theory. *Career Choice and Development* (4th ed., 255–311).

15. Maria Mitchell Association. (n.d.). *About Maria Mitchell* [Foundation]. Maria Mitchell Association. Retrieved May 16, 2020, from https://www.mariamitchell.org/about/about-maria-mitchell

16. Milligan, S. (2017). *Stepping through history*. U.S. News and World Report. https://www.usnews.com/news/the-report/articles/2017-01-20/timeline-the-womens-rights-movement-in-the-us

17. National Academies of Sciences, Engineering, and Medicine. (2018). *Sexual harassment of women: Climate, culture, and consequences in academic sciences, engineering, and medicine*. Washington, DC: The National Academies Press. https://doi.org/10.17226/24994.

18. *NSF Director France A. Córdova Biography*. (n.d.). NSF – National Science Foundation. Retrieved May 16, 2020, from https://www.nsf.gov/news/speeches/cordova/cordova_bio.jsp

19. Okahana, H., & Zhou, E. (2019). *Graduate Enrollment and Degrees: 2008 to 2018*.

20. Orenstein, D. (2013, October 4). *Wiki editing recognizes women in science*. Brown University. https://news.brown.edu/articles/2013/10/lovelace

21. Pappas, S. (2013, March 6). *5 reasons women trail men in science*. Live Science. https://www.livescience.com/27682-women-men-science-gender-gap.html

22. *Research and Trends for Women in STEM – Society of Women Engineers*. (n.d.). Research and Trends for Women in STEM. Retrieved May 17, 2020, from https://research.swe.org/

23. Roberts, J. (2015, February 11). *NASA Astronaut Dr. Ellen Ochoa* [Text]. NASA. http://www.nasa.gov/centers/johnson/about/people/orgs/bios/ochoa.html

24. Rossiter, M. W. (1982). *Women scientists in America: Struggles and strategies to 1940* (Vol. 1). Johns Hopkins University Press Books.

25. Rossiter, M. W. (1993). The Matthew Matilda effect in science. *Social Studies of Science, 23*(2), 325–341. JSTOR.

26. Rossiter, M. W. (1998). *Women scientists in America: Before affirmative action, 1940–1972* (Vol. 2). Johns Hopkins University Press Books.

27. Roy, J. (2019). *Engineering by numbers engineering statistics* (p. 40). American Society for Engineering Education. http://www.asee.org/documents/papers-and-publications/publications/college-profiles/2018-Engineering-by-Numbers-Engineering-Statistics-UPDATED-15-July-2019.pdf

28. Science & Government Report. (1989, May 15). *The San Francisco Examiner*, 32.
29. Seitz, F. (n.d.). *A selection of highlights from the history of the National Academy of Sciences, 1863–2005*. National Academy of Sciences. Retrieved May 16, 2020, from http://www.nasonline.org/about-nas/history/highlights/
30. Super, D. E. (1980). A life-span, life-space approach to career development. *Journal of Vocational Behavior, 16*(3), 282–298. https://doi.org/10.1016/0001-8791(80)90056-1.
31. *SWOCC*. (n.d.). STEM Women of Color Conclave. Retrieved May 16, 2020, from https://www.conclave-swoc.net/about
32. The Editors of Encyclopaedia Britannica. (2020). Matilda Joslyn Gage. In *Encyclopedia Britannica*. Encyclopædia Britannica, Inc. https://www.britannica.com/biography/Matilda-Joslyn-Gage
33. Weiler, N. (2014, July 30). *Lydia Villa-Komaroff Learned in the Lab "What It Might Be Like to Fly."* The American Society of Cell Biology. https://www.ascb.org/member-news/lydia-villa-komaroff-learned-in-the-lab-what-it-might-be-like-to-fly/
34. *Women, Minorities, and Persons with Disabilities in Science and Engineering: 2019 | NSF – National Science Foundation*. (2019, March 8). https://ncses.nsf.gov/pubs/nsf19304/
35. Cook, E. P., Heppner, M. J., & O'Brien, K. M. (2002). Career development of women of color and White women: Assumptions, conceptualization, and interventions from an ecological perspective. *The Career Development Quarterly, 50*(4), 291–305.

Chapter 2
Feminist Psychology and Sociocultural Precipitants to Women's Leadership

The Emergence of Feminism and Feminist Psychology

Chapter 1 discussed the role of activism principally by women that led to new laws that empowered women to vote, work, and be protected in educational access through Title IX. Women leaders who advocated for legislation to empower women resisted the oppressive societal structures and policies. At times they were punished for their advocacy, but their values and goals were for the collective good of women, not for individual gain. Persistence is evident in the work of feminists of the past and the present.

Feminist psychology came into being to provide a different narrative in psychology, not only about gender and sex differences but to elevate the science by and about women. Feminists and feminism are not new globally nor in the USA. Depending on the source one uses to identify historical and contemporary feminist theorists and activists, it is generally not very long. In this section, there will be a discussion of first-, second-, and third-fourth-wave feminists and parallels of their advocacy to the evolution of feminist psychology.

First-Wave Feminists

Among first-wave feminists is Mary Wollstonecraft (1759–1797), a British feminist philosopher. In her 1792 landmark article, "A Vindication of the Rights of Women," she criticized Rousseau's writings about women's inferiority [76]. A second historical example is Sojourner Truth (1797–1883), who stands out as a suffragist and abolitionist, who through self-determination was freed from slavery in 1827. She was born as Isabella Baumfree but in 1843 claimed her identity as Sojourner Truth, saying God decreed it. She was the first African American to win a lawsuit, freeing her enslaved son. Sojourner Truth was a true social justice advocate crusading on behalf of slaves, women and African Americans [46]

Susan B. Anthony (1820–1906) is often heralded because she was the first woman whose image appeared on a US coin. Like other first-wave feminists, she pushed on the boundaries designed to keep women out of civic life and privileges that were undisputed for white men. She was a leader in the anti-slavery and suffragist movement. Reportedly, she was arrested for illegally voting in the presidential election of 1872.

A French Feminist-Bridging First- and Second-Wave Feminists

An intellectual, philosopher, and feminist, Simone de Beauvoir wrote about and advocated for recognizing women as beings independent of their sexuality and meriting a vocation equal to men. In *The Second Sex* [8], she discusses the historical treatment of women, positing that women are always the "other" and men the default and in superior positions. She often described women as enslaved as depicted in artwork, literature, and through laws that subjugate a woman because of her sex. Beauvoir contrasts a girl's upbringing with a boy's, who at age 3 or 4 is told he is a "little man" ([9], pp 285–286). A girl is taught to be a woman, and her "feminine" destiny is imposed on her by society ([9], pp 294–295).

This statement resonates with Margaret Rossiter's findings on the existence of women scientists. Women were not considered equal and often relegated to the role of assistant to the man. They were the "second sex" or the omitted sex as occurred with women not included when awards were given, including the Nobel Prize. Simone de Beauvoir, in many ways, bridged the two waves of feminism.

Second-Wave Feminism

Second-wave feminism (1960–1980s) is primarily associated with activism in the USA. President Kennedy established the first Commission on the Status of Women and appointed Eleanor Roosevelt to lead it in 1961. Equality was crucial for issues that the Commission addressed, recommending equality in employment opportunities, pay, and childcare. Their work led to the Equal Pay Act of 1963 [16] that was later amended through the Civil Rights Act of 1964 that prohibited employers from discrimination against women based on sex. This period also saw a new type of literature from women advocating for a work identity, marriage where they were not tied to the kitchen, and open dialogue about sexuality.

In *Sexual Politics* [61], Kate Millet argued that all politics involved power-structured relationships. Betty Friedan, the co-founder of the National Organization for Women, posited in *The Feminine Mystique* [40] that women enacted their roles as wives and mothers, although it was not their preference. By so doing, they were demonstrating their femininity and fulfilling the stereotypes expected of women.

Friedan asserted that women could be feminine without assuming the roles ascribed to them, challenging the traditional gender-bound portrayals of women in all mediums [21]. Another notable white feminist is Gloria Steinem, the founder and editor of *MS* magazine (1976). A journalist and social justice activist, she has consistently championed women's rights nationally and internationally. She believes in women's self-determination regarding abortion and other limitations imposed on women socially and has expressed feminist viewpoints through many books and essays (History.com Editors, 2018). Her book, *Moving Beyond Words: Age, Rage, Sex, Power, Money, Muscles: Breaking the Boundaries of Gender* (1994), includes essays including one that challenges Freud's sexist views of women.

The women's liberation movement, as it came to be called, emboldened a sector of white women in the USA. Before long, it was seen as a movement that excluded lower-income women and women of color. African American women contended that not only were they excluded because of sex, but they also had the race factor against them. The most outspoken critics were writers such as bell hooks, Alice Walker, and Bettina Aptheker [16]. During this same period, the 1960s–1980s, Dolores Huerta, of Mexican-American heritage, was a leading activist on behalf of agricultural workers' rights, issues of women workers, and other disenfranchised groups in the country. She co-established the National Farmworkers Union with César Chávez. She does not appear among the names of second-wave feminists ironically.

The common denominator among many second-wave feminists is that they were adults in the decades when traditional roles for women as stay-at-home mothers and wives were the norm. Nevertheless, their worldview was much greater, motivating their advocacy for women's participation in politics and the workplace and examining women's voice in matters of sexuality and the family. Second-wave feminists gave voice to women's rights through literature, activism, and other public fora [15]. Even today, the voices of Gloria Steinem, Dolores Huerta, and celebrities such as Jane Fonda and Lily Tomlin provide leadership on social justice issues.

Third-Wave Feminists

Third-wave feminism began in the 1990s, primarily by women from Boomer and Generation X, who were beneficiaries of the advances of the civil rights movement, including Title IX legislation. They emphasized individualism and diversity, stating they believed these concepts were overlooked by the women's liberation movement and early women feminists. It is reported that the term "third-wave feminist" was the title of an essay by Rebecca Walker, a bisexual African American woman from Mississippi. She argued that women who were not heterosexual nor white were excluded from feminism; however, this began to change in the 1990s through scholarship and activism [1].

Diversity, equity, and inclusive identities became pervasive themes among third-wave feminists. In a landmark article, Kimberlé Crenshaw, an African American legal scholar, coined the term "intersectionality" to describe the oppression experienced by African American women. In a 2018 talk to the New York Women's Foundation, Crenshaw pointed out that her premise from 1989 holds today; women's identities, particularly for women of color, cannot be limited to one identity category. She also allowed that intersectionality is not limited to black women but also applies to other individuals whose identities are marginalized by any one of our social identities [68, 74].

Third-wave feminists tended to be scholars, using their academic platforms to argue for postmodern issues such as gender on a continuum, establishment of more gender studies programs, and openness of behaviors and identities that are not gender conforming nor representative of stereotyped women. These Generation X women and others classified as Baby Boomers continue to lead discourse about equity in higher education spaces, including the sciences and engineering.

Third-wave feminism has brought to the fore activism by women as demonstrated in the #metoo movement, visible support of political candidates, demonstrations for sociopolitical causes such as reproductive rights, and political office candidacy. In the first year of the #metoo movement launch, the Equal Employment Opportunity Commission saw a 50% increase in sexual harassment charges filed from the previous year [20]. In the November 2018 elections, a record number of women were elected to Congress [27]. Attributes across the group were their younger age; ethnic, racial, and cultural diversity; and willingness to confront the status quo [27].

Black Feminists

Black women always gave voice to issues of inequities along with their white sisters and independently. For the causes they championed had to do with racism as well as sexism, discrimination and prejudice based on color, and outright hostility because they were black. Black feminists did not ask for permission. They made their way into conversations about feminism in academic and political spaces; three are highlighted here. bell hooks is one of the most acclaimed black feminists, challenging white supremacy and male patriarchy. Her first book at age 19 was *Ain't I a Woman, Black Women, and Feminism* [51]. Her book's title is based on the famous speech *Ain't I a Woman* by Sojourner Truth in 1851 at the Women's Rights Convention in Akron, Ohio. In *Feminist Theory: Margin to Center* [52], she writes critically about the limited scope of feminism written by white women. Audre Lorde is another critical voice in the black feminist movement. A lesbian, mother, and poet, through her writing and activism, she challenged injustices of sexism, racism, and homophobia and the marginalization of black lesbian women. Not as widely known in academic circles as Lorde and hooks is Frances Beal. The daughter of a Jewish father and African American mother fought against anti-Semitism, sexism, racism, and racial justice. Her most well-known publication was *Double Jeopardy: To Be Black and Female* [7]. She discussed how Black women's intersecting identities were a constant struggle in a racist society. To achieve liberation, she asserted, women had to fight back, raise their voices, and not accept subjugation based on color and gender.

Feminist Psychology and the Psychology of Women

Feminist psychology is considered a form of psychology that has persisted in counterpointing the profession's dominant male biases. Feminists challenge existing systems, theories, and practices grounded in White male patriarchy and objectivity without considering sociohistorical and sociocultural contexts. The origins of feminist psychology point to Karen Horney (1885–1952), a psychoanalyst and physician of Dutch-German heritage. She is known for her work on child development, positing that the cultural environment/attitudes influence children's socialization and the development of neuroses. Dr. Horney's theory of neurosis is described as a means to cope with fears as a part of normal life. Among the ten neuroses, she posits the need for power, affection, independence, and prestige [19]. A neo-Freudian, she objected to Freud's descriptions of women's psychology, particularly that of penis envy as demeaning. Instead, she posited it was "womb envy" that was in play, fueling men's insecurities because they could not have children. Horney was a prolific writer, advancing perspectives about the role of sociocultural and environmental contexts on people's development [73] later introduced by multicultural psychology and women of color scholars [2, 3, 25, 44] and cultural-relational theorists and psychotherapists [19]. Among Horney's classic texts are *Feminine Psychology* [54] and *The Collected Works of Karen Horney (Volume II)* [53].

Also leading the voice of feminists was Dr. Jean Baker Miller (1929–1994), a psychiatrist and leading researcher on women's psychological development through the Stone Center at Wellesley College. Her groundbreaking book, *Toward a New Psychology of Women* (1976), introduced issues women faced based on our socialization with lesser social status imposed by dominant groups. She discussed problems of domination and subordination and temporary and permanent inequality as conditions that primarily affect women and those considered to be less equal to the dominant group, i.e., White men.

Most so-called women's work is not recognized as real activity. One reason for this attitude may be that such work is usually associated with helping others' development, rather than with self-enhancement or self-employment [60].

Miller also discussed conflicts women have about power and the fear of using it. Most often, she wrote, women have been taught to avoid power because it does not support femininity or other stereotyped perceptions about women.

Psychology of Women

The psychology of women as a field of study has evolved since the 1970s with the founding of two feminist organizations—Association of Women Psychologists (1969) and the Society for the Psychology of Women, Division 35 (1974) of the American Psychological Association (APA)—and women's studies program in universities. The journal *Feminist Theory* in 1990 opened up different perspectives on feminism and its theory. It is a critical stance toward sociopolitical and essential change. The *Psychology of Women Quarterly*, established in 1976 and published by APA Division 35, addresses specifics to women's health from multiple perspectives, including women's studies, and psychological aspects of women's well-being. Division 35 has attracted women of different cultural heritages through five specific sections, thereby addressing intersecting priorities for each section and also advancing women of color in the role of division presidents. It addresses and advocates for multiple social justice issues affecting primarily women in work settings and relationships. The scholarship that has emerged over the last 40 years places a spotlight on the need to contextualize issues that affect women's empowerment, psychological development, and self-determination. Science by and about women addresses domestic violence, the effects of trauma on mental well-being, and the role of spirituality as a strength. This scholarship's value is that it underscores the complexity of women's lives from various identity and lifespan perspectives in male-dominated societies, systems, and institutions.

Teaching the psychology of women also began in the late 1970s, particularly in university women's studies programs. The latter are interdisciplinary with curriculum typically addressing feminist theory, multiculturalism, social justice, and women's intersecting identities. Systems of oppression and privilege and the role of power in social and cultural contexts as these relate to women are examined [77]. Women's studies programs also foster identity affirmation, the practices of collectivism and relational-cultural theory among students and faculty, and give imagination and permission to new research lines benefitting women.

There are several psychology of women texts that have become the most widely recognized for their comprehensive approach to discussing various aspects of women's psychological development [29, 30, 31, 35, 75]. With each updated text, there is a presentation of more integrated topics such as gender, ethnicity, sexual orientation, and socioeconomic status within structurally biased systems. The term intersectionality is now commonplace and threaded throughout these anthologies. These are primarily edited texts in which contributors write on a topic of their expertise, such as personality development; sexuality; multiple identities; career development; social psychology constructs such as stigma, stereotype threat, and marginalization; and systems. These continue to be barriers to women's access and opportunities across higher learning institutions, political offices, and other industries. These texts are grounded in feminist principles and practices designed to create and implement equity, recognition, and respect for women's experiences in their given discipline.

In the sections that follow, attention will be given to theories on women's identity development, socialization theory as it applies to women's psychological development and empowerment, and feminine development across the lifecycle with attention to cultural differences. We recognize that these are broad topics and that entire books can be devoted to each topic. However, we intend to continue to put forth contextual, developmental, and cultural backdrops for women in general and women in STEM, in particular.

Different Perspectives on the Psychology of Women's Development

Women's sense of cultural and gender identity is grounded in historic sociopolitical biases and cultural values and practices about women's roles in a given society [24, 37]. Being second-class citizens or lesser than has been challenged by feminists as they advanced thinking about equitable access and opportunities for women of previous generations [5, 8]. In a review of women's status in more than 50 countries, Arredondo [5] found similar patterns of oppression and discrimination of women. In some cultures, women walk behind the men. In others, the young wives move into the husband's home and take care of his family, and in other situations, women may not divorce for fear of death. Growing up with messages that one is less than a man or a male child is not imagined by girls. Rather, these messages about deficit status and other deficiencies are introduced by their families and become internalized and liabilities as they move into schools, universities, and the workplace. There are always exceptions to these repressive societal practices and leadership by women that benefit the collective, going beyond their gain. A few examples will be shared.

For her advocacy for children's education, Malala Yousafzai, at age 17, became the youngest Nobel Prize Laureate in 2014. From Pakistan, she was strident in her activism for children's rights to attend schools, though the Taliban viciously pursued her. At age 32, Mairead Corrigan was awarded the Nobel Peace Prize for leading the Northern Ireland Peace Movement, composed primarily of women. The organization sought to bring about peace between the Catholics and Protestants in Northern Ireland. In the USA, Mothers Against Drunk Driving is another example of activism that benefits others. At age 92, Dolores Huerta continues her social justice activism on behalf of children's education, LGBTQ individuals, immigrant agricultural families, and other disenfranchised groups.

Theories and Perspectives on Women's Psychological Development

Influenced by the feminist movement unfolding at the turn of the twentieth century, Carl Jung outlined psychological differentiation between men and women [69] and developed terms to describe these differences. He discussed the development of masculine and feminine attributes as masculine and feminine archetypes, known as "psychic imprints," that are inborn patterns of experiencing or sensing. In Jungian theory, the actualization of one's potential relies upon the development of the contra-sexual archetype. In other words, men and women work to harmonize their masculine and feminine aspects to reach fulfillment. The archetype of the feminine is known as the anima, while the archetype of the masculine is known as the animus. Jung described the anima as the feminine principle comprising relatedness, the inferior, feeling, intuition, cooperation, and nurturing. The animus, per Jung, is composed of aggression, cognition, rationality, focusing, structure, competition, and hierarchy. Interestingly, these are many of the same stereotyped attributes used to differentiate women and men in different cultural contexts. It has been argued that the Jungian perspective of women's development is limited and serves as another theoretical viewpoint of misunderstanding women's development [26].

A theory of feminine development across the lifecycle was developed as a counterpoint to male-focused experiences that so often pervaded influences in psychotherapy practice. Eight phases account for a re-experiencing of any given phase as life progresses, including accounting for a deepening level of awareness, capability, and integration [26]. Descriptions of the phases in brief follow:

Phase 1: Bonding: A special relationship forms between a daughter and a mother.

Phase 2: Orientation Toward Others: Early on, a girl learns about role expectations as she is socialized to attend to the wants, feelings, and needs of others.

Phase 3: Cultural Adaptation: Becoming a "pseudo-man," emerging from hyper-adaptability skills gained by girls.

Phase 4: Awakening and Separation: In the adolescent years, girls experience confusion about relationships and dissatisfaction with oneself as others may judge women as stepping out of line or not role-congruent.

Phase 5: The Development of the Feminine: An effort to move to trust one's intuitive knowledge and sit with one's self and feelings.

Phase 6: Empowerment: This phase symbolizes the exertion of a woman's will or self-determination in a male-dominated world.

Phase 7: Spiritual Development: The evolved woman she becomes, through courage, incorporates her healing or spiritual potential.

Phase 8: Integration: Opportunities present themselves for discernment on the use of masculine and feminine energies.

Women's psychological development is not linear, static, nor defined by a checklist to describe what happens at different ages or pre- and post-menstruation, nor defined by her capacity to bear children. In a classic article, Carol Gilligan wrote *In a Different Voice: Psychological Theory and Women's Development* [41], addressing differences in the reasoning processes for boys and girls. A moral development scholar, she began to question how the moral development schema suggested that male children had a more evolved cognitive process when faced with hypothetical ethical dilemmas. The famous case involves the dilemma about a child stealing a drug because a family member was dying. The boy was going to resort to an authoritative conflictual, hierarchical approach to win the situation. At the same time, the young girl considered the relationships involved and how this led her to try to resolve the dilemma. So often, Gilligan contended, boys reasoned through the mindset of winning or losing. Girls, alternatively, were taught how to relate, consider others, and problem-solve situations. This is the different reasoning approach women often bring to problematic workplace situations.

Women's Ways of Knowing [10] addresses women's cognitive processes for developing and sharing knowledge through five positions or perspectives. The researchers conducted a study with 135 women from different ethnic, age, socioeconomic class, educational history, and urban and rural settings. While Gilligan addressed moral development reasoning, Belenky and her colleagues focused on self-conception, relationship with others, and how women came to understand authority. The five ways of knowing were categorized as *silence, received knowledge: listening to the voices of others, subjective knowledge or the inner voice, procedural knowledge: separate and connected knowing, and constructed knowing: integrating the voices.* As standpoint theory [47, 48] would explain, positionality contributes to knowledge creation. As Belenky et al. found in their study, women come to know through different processes, relational but also in relation to oneself. In short, women can engage in abstract thinking, self-reflect, give voice to others, connect the dots when it comes to making sense of situations, and balance multiple perspectives.

The Psychology of Women of Color

To discuss the psychology of women may suggest that all women fit into the same shoebox. This is far from the case. As was previously reviewed, Black women feminists did not believe the feminist movement was about them. Further, it is argued that not only was the second wave of feminism led by White women primarily of the upper-middle class, but it also ignored women of ethnic and racial minority backgrounds who had historically been discriminated against and marginalized based on both gender and race. Though chapters on women of color appear in the psychology of women texts, other books written by and about women of color have provided essential knowledge.

In *Psychological Health of Women of Color: Intersections, Challenges, and Opportunities*, Comas-Diaz and Greene [24] present an anthology, a published collection, addressing challenges of emotional well-being faced by women of color in a racist society. Intersectionality is introduced by focused attention to lesbian women of color, multiracial women, immigrant women of color, and women with disabilities. Attention is also given to professional women and their achievements and leadership. The anthology contributors are a cross section of women of color who can provide a voice from their lived experiences and intersecting dimensions of identity navigating spaces that are often not welcoming. It is notable that despite experiences of hostility, they persist. The anthology serves a collective effort, giving voice to a variety of backgrounds and allowing for shared empowerment, highlighting a difference from an individualistic approach common in Western psychology.

In the *Oxford Handbook of Feminist Multicultural Psychology* [37], a four-volume anthology, particular attention is given to experiences of women from different cultural backgrounds internationally and domestically. The contributors write from their own experiences, in particular, providing person-person narratives. A chapter on feminist multicultural psychology posits the need to not separate culture, gender, sexuality, age, and ability from gender. When it comes to women, all of these social identities are of lower status; thus, it is up to women to relate "herstory" to advance equity not only in psychology but in other disciplines and life spaces, including professional women's associations.

Feminist multicultural psychology is a concept introduced by counseling psychologists, a professional domain of applied psychology. More specifically and relevant to feminist worldviews is that counseling psychology's values are (a) strengths-based, emphasizing dignity and diversity, resilience, and "optimal" well-being; (b) about a lifespan approach to human development with attention to careers, educational, and personal needs of individuals; (c) giving attention to societal macro- and microsystems that affect human development; (d) education and prevention for health enhancement; (e) advocacy and social justice principles and practices; and (f) collaborative practices that promote equity, multidisciplinary networks, and different sources of knowledge, including personal narratives [37]. Feminist multicultural psychology advances strengths-based inclusionary premises that remove the limits from historic feminist psychology. This primarily addresses white women and acknowledges that women from different cultural backgrounds have unique lived experiences that deepen and enrich feminist psychology literature.

Standpoint Theory

The concept of positionality continually emerges in discussions about women's determination to claim our own space and voice in the face of persistent sociopolitical barriers that limit our access based on sexism, racism, and classism. To this end, the concept of standpoint theory was developed by Sandra Harding, an American feminist theorist, to "categorize epistemologies that emphasize women's knowledge" [13]. Harding asserts that in the pyramid model of social hierarchies, scholars at the top lose sight of the experiences of those further down and miss out on multiple social realities they do not live. As a result, those marginalized have a more authentic view for developing inclusive scholarship that explains many sociocultural issues and everyday problems. This is exemplified by the scholarship of Horney, Miller, and other women who point to men's characterization of women as less than in multiple contexts and settings, writing from their privileged experiences.

Further, men tend to promote objectivity versus subjectivity, thereby overlooking the complexity of human relations and other life challenges. Dorothy Smith, a sociologist, also asserted that sociologists need to begin their research from women's experiences and perspectives to understand why they/we have always been objectified as the other [66]. Women's roles as caregivers are taken for granted and set aside while men are glorified to pursue their objective and abstract ideas, not grounded in lived experiences.

Standpoint theorists also question the reliance on the methodology that is purported to be objective and neutral. In so doing, these scientists also perpetuate linear, noncomplex thinking that is ahistorical and acontextual. Clearly, this does not fit feminist ways of knowing. Harding believes that methodology that is inclusive of marginalized people and women will likely create knowledge that is more relevant and applicable more broadly.

Also raising her voice in the standpoint theory discussion is Patricia Hill Collins, who wrote about Black feminist thought and the politics of empowerment [22]. She pointed to the matrix of oppression—race, class, gender, and privilege—experienced by African American women that provides particular perspectives to understand their marginalization, economic exploitation, and stereotyping by those who are privileged. According to Fiske [39], those with privilege control stereotyping and impose othering labels, rendering those they oppress not to have a voice. When this occurs, according to Collins, women or the other are objectified and dehumanized by researchers. Standpoint theory goes beyond the focus on women but also embraces the perspectives of those from different marginalized positions. In this text, we move away from the objectification of STEM women from diverse backgrounds and intersecting identities to demonstrate the complexity of their lived experiences.

Standpoint theory also enters into discussions about communications and how power and privilege are wielded by those in positions of authority and/or power. Although sharing of one's opinion or attitude can be called standpoint, this still comes back to perceptions based on positionality and appreciating or denigrating one's viewpoint based on their marginalized status. Tannen [71] cites how men use their positionality in workplace situations to silence women and attempt to reduce them or disqualify their perspectives. A powerful example emerged in July 2020 when Congresswoman Alexandria Ocasio-Cortez (AOC) challenged the verbal insults of a senior White male Congressman who publicly called her a "f… bitch." In her retort, AOC cited the man's positionality and that of all men believe they can insult women and hide behind their relationships with their wives and daughters. In her speech, AOC spoke for women of all backgrounds who are visibly disrespected by men in power.

Women's Multiple and Intersecting Identities

Pigeon-holing women into one sexed-based category historically has put severe limitations on the roles and expectations of women and contributed to negative stereotyping and biases. Moreover, the single category of "women" has overlooked the multiple identities a woman holds. Discussions about women of different cultural and ethnic backgrounds in varying scientific professions and occupations and as leaders, as two examples, are often met with surprise and even bewilderment. In 2020, there are still prevailing assumptions about women's competence to be leaders and scientists and often even more bewilderment when these are women of color, mothers, or women with disabilities. Women's identities are complex and intersecting, as will be discussed in the next section.

Women's Dimensions of Personal, Intersecting Identities

The Dimensions of Personal Identity (DPI) model [4, 6] provides an historical and sociocultural framework to ground multiple intersectional dimensions of an individual's identity. The DPI outlines three intersecting and interdependent identity domains, the A, B, and C dimensions (see Fig. 2.1). As illustrated in Dimension A,

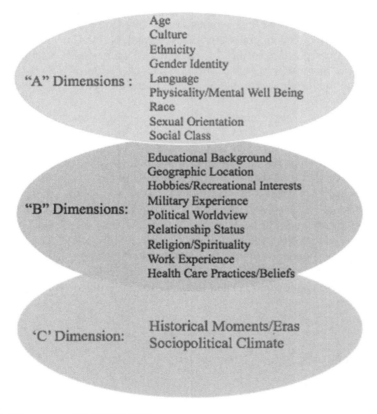

Fig. 2.1 Dimensions of Personal Identity
Note: The A dimension can have positive and negative valences, which impact self-concept, self-esteem, and empowerment, and they are the least changeable. The B dimensions are less visible and are developmental in nature. The C dimensions emphasize historical contexts and external forces that individuals and families must deal with though these are not in their control

gender is but one of several dimensions of identity and includes ethnicity and race, culture, age, sexual orientation, language, and socioeconomic status. These are characterized as "fixed" or less fluid dimensions of identity, endowed at birth, and not readily altered. As is evident, the global term woman does not capture all of the other identities a woman carries. As Crenshaw wrote [28], African American women are visible because of their gender and race. Further, Helms [49] discussed Visible Ethnic Racial Groups (VERG) and the challenges for individuals like women of Asian and Black identity because of their visibility of color and other phenotypic characteristics. Though color is not identified in the A dimensions, it is a part of one's identity.

The B dimension includes dimensions of identity that one may choose, earn, or arrive at through different developmental and life experiences. Applying the B dimensions to women in STEM, it is apparent that there will be a range of differences that contribute to self-appraisal and appraisals and attributions from others. For example, (a) women's educational experiences will vary based on the STEM discipline (biology versus engineering) they are in, the institutional home of their doctoral degree, and their scope of research; (b) work experience and the type of institution where they hold a position, lecturer versus tenure track, will also inform attributions about them; (c) relationship status often comes up for women balancing families and career goals with assumptions made about their career commitment if they have children; (d) geographic location also plays a role in a woman's identity; place of birth, location for work, and mobility opportunities may affect her work identity, status, and successes. Although the B dimensions are typically not visible as are the A dimensions, there are still biases that may emerge, say, from search committees and editorial review boards based on some of the B dimensions that appear on a curriculum vitae.

Through this brief description, it should also be notable that STEM women's experiences will also be affected by their A dimensions, more specifically, ethnicity, race, sexual orientation, and age. A light-skinned Puerto Rican Latina with a degree in chemistry from Yale will likely be perceived differently from a Puerto Rican Afro-Latina with an electrical engineering degree from the University of Florida.

The C dimension of identity refers to historical eras and moments, significant events, or experiences that have marked a woman's life and career. For example, COVID-19 in 2020 may have interrupted an academic's research, complicating her tenure planning process. The pandemic has also required mothers to do home-schooling. Research indicates that male university faculty are the beneficiaries of the stay-at-home policies during the COVID period. In fact, their scholarly submissions increased during this period compared to those of women [38].

The killings of Black individuals in the USA in 2020 placed additional pressure on Black women in STEM. As mothers of boys or adolescents, they carry additional stress about their sons' well-being. Further, depending on the career status of a woman when major sociocultural incidents occur such as the 2008 Recession, #metoo movement, #Black Lives Matter, and the COVID-19 epidemic, the pressures may increase because of family responsibilities, economic pressures, and university priorities to publish and continue to teach and advise students. Health can also be compromised as women of color balance multiple personal and professional priorities while their tenure clock continues to tick.

The Dimensions of Personal Identity model highlights the complexity of women's visible, invisible, and intersecting identities. Attributions based on women's visible identities, family status, age, and domestic versus international cultural heritage, as a few examples, are out of a woman's control. Yet, negative assumptions and attributions may persist. In a society that does not overtly value the intelligence and accomplishments of women, there are continuous challenges to self-esteem and self-efficacy. Moreover, in the academy, the dynamics of institutional racism and sexism continue to affect women's status, power, and privilege. It is still a dominant White man's domain with historic policies for promotion and tenure that benefit men. Perhaps in time, a historic moment will be the creation of promotion and tenure guidelines designed by women.

Adverse Identity Self-Perceptions

In *Women & Self-Esteem*, the authors [65] contend that with the high regard for men and the depreciation of women, it is no wonder that women's egos tailspin downward. How women think about themselves influences their emotions and their feelings about themselves. The combination of the negative cognitive and emotional processes contributes to a lack of confidence in a woman's sense of competency, skills, and capabilities, adequacy, and doubts about being lovable. The most significant threats to women's self-esteem per Sanford and Donavan are self-perceptions about a lack of significance, that they matter and competence, that they are capable of "performing," and how these are reinforced in family relationships, institutions, and work settings. These challenges to women's self-regard and self-esteem are complex and need to be understood as not emanating from a woman's negative thinking, but from the broader contexts in which she has been socialized. The descriptions provided in *Women & Self-Esteem* relate directly to impostorism and stereotype threat.

Imposter Syndrome While the imposter phenomenon affects women in the workforce, there is a particular experience affecting women in STEM. Tao and Gloria [72] asked a sample of 224 women graduate students to disclose their experience of imposter characteristics to find a confirmation of their hypothesis that the greater its perception, the lower a grasp on self-efficacy, a decrease in positive views of their academic context, and lesser optimistic viewing of obtaining their doctorate. In this study, attitudes about persistence were mediated by the level of belief in one's ability and perceptions of the doctoral environment [72]. This research highlights a relationship between feeling like a fraud and the stance to carry on anyway. As more women are represented in the doctoral environment, the relationship is strengthened [72]. It seems as though the imposter syndrome experience is divisive, however. It might be useful to understand perceptions of where this experience derives. That is, how early does a sense of impostorism set in and what contexts. Is it always in education settings?

A longitudinal study that may be applicable to understand underrepresented groups further examined the relationship between first-generation students' valuing of commonality and collaboration and the competitive culture in courses, and the impact on feelings of being an imposter daily [17]. It was hypothesized that classroom competition might be a barrier to the promotion of this sample's success in the STEM field. Particularly, more research focusing on the etiology of real-time classroom experiences of women with a wide array of variables that contribute to a misperception of failure will give clear direction as a means to resolving the perceptions of division.

A meta-analysis of 62 publications related to prevalence, comorbidity, or treatment of the imposter syndrome conducted over the years 1990–2018 found a recent increase in interest on the topic as evidenced by over half of the analyzed studies taking place over the most recent 6 years [14]. It is further noted through more general research that while this experience affects women, it is prominent within the entire population to the extent that it has not been found to fully account for the range in experiences of women in the STEM field [14].

Stereotype Threat Multiple factors have been explored to account for learning and implementing strategies for empowering women in STEM careers. Women in STEM are at risk of confirming the stereotype threat that they are inferior in performance [11]. When women, as a minority representation of engineers, believe they set the baseline intelligence for women in all STEM education, they are faced with the threat of confirming that their intelligence alone is indicative of all women in the field [11]. This stereotype threat exacerbates the perception of pressure in a field with a higher demand for women's advancement [63], thus increasing susceptibility to its experience. The negative result of this phenomenon may be contributing to a slow rate of retention of diverse faculty and a lack of ability to meet the increasing demands in full participation. The existence of this phenomenon in African Americans requires further examination as institutions pursue the hiring and retention of these faculty women [63, 67].

A paradoxical effect was reported in research indicating that specific individuals may be motivated to disconfirm notions of stereotype threat, placing pressure on working memory resulting in performance suffering [55, 63]. It takes cognitive effort to process information; when a cognitive effort is exerted on processing information associated with negative stereotypes, performance is negatively affected [55].

Another study examined systemic stereotype threat and how women navigate their careers within persistent adverse systems. "Systemic stereotype threat occurs when an individual is in a system that is characterized by gender or racial disparities and the implicit belief about the reason for these disparities is stereotypes about the deficits of women or people of color, rather than systemic inequalities" ([12], p. 33). Through interviews with 26 women scientists in top-tier research universities, the researchers identified 3 types of response patterns the women used to navigate their careers. These were classified as *fending off the threat, confronting the threat, and sustaining self in the presence of the threat* ([12], p. 34). The findings point to the responsibility placed on the women to manage and deal with the threats on an individual basis. An institutional response is rarely forthcoming, nor are there systems to support women in their drives for accomplishment, self-efficacy, and success.

Leadership by Women Through Feminist Perspectives and Experiences

Leadership paradigms taught in business and higher education leadership programs primarily derive from male models. For many years, Theory X and Theory Y leaders have been touted as the ideal leaders [58, 59] to be emulated. Given men's socialization for competition and control, the premise of these models is that leaders be autocratic and exert command-and-control style behavior, militaristic behavior. With women socialized to be nurturers, social beings, and collaborators versus top-down styles of leading, expectations about male-like behavior pose possible intrapersonal challenges. Often, those familiar with traditional leading models will be critical of a woman's style of leading, or if she leads "like a man," there may be a criticism of role incongruity. As discussed in the previous paragraphs, hiring women as department chairs may score DEI points for the university administration, but this does not mean it is a smooth process because it is disruptive to the status quo.

Multiple alternatives to the commanding male model that emerged were the situation leadership [50] and relational-cultural theory that describe a style of leading [57] and growing through relationships or coexistence. These are seen as more person-centered, collaborative, and less transactional styles of leadership. Through women-centered research, descriptions of women's styles of leadership have also emerged. Terms such as collectivistic, interactive, coach, and teacher-like practices pointed to women leading in ways that were more people-centered and participatory [18].

Culture-specific and feminist models for leading have also been introduced. Eagly and Chin [32] addressed the omission of persons of color in leadership and the loss to organizations when individuals with multiple experiences and perspectives are not considered for leadership roles. They indicate that going beyond traditional leader models will enhance and give a greater breadth of thought in an organization. The Osah Gan Gio model [56] is an indigenous model that describes five roles for leaders in higher education. These roles are: "sharing a commitment to serve their community, claiming their voices for themselves and their community, demonstrated and modeled ways that education is key to cultural survival and self-determination, traveling across boundaries to understand and bridge relationships with others who are different from themselves, and continuously nurturing their inner spirit and sustaining their soul through balance in their lives" ([62], p. 3). The concept of *mujerista* refers to feminist Latinas who seek liberation and self-determination on their terms. The *mujerista* worldview also introduces perspectives of women's strengths, resilience, self-expression, and self-determination with women leaders. Always present for *mujeristas* is the value of relationships [23].

Role congruity theory [33, 34] has also been researched concerning women in leadership roles and the notion that men are expected to be dominant as leaders. Alternatively, because of stereotypes, women are expected to be communal versus agentic. Agentic leadership refers to a style of behavior that demonstrates assertiveness, independence, courage, and competitiveness, coming from business environments typically associated with men. In terms of role congruity theory, "when women do exhibit agentic behaviors they are evaluated as less communal because they are perceived to have violated their gender role expectations" ([64], p. 221). Agentic leadership efficacy (ALE) was researched as a model for development and performance [45]. In his study, Hannah found that a leader's self-schema adapts over time based on an increased sense of self-efficacy, confidence in her or his leadership skills, and sustained performance within a specific leadership area. It was also found that ALE can be developed through a targeted leadership development program.

In the domain of women's leadership, attention has also been given to prejudice toward women leaders, as explained by role congruity theory. The "perceived incongruity between the female gender role and leadership roles leads to two forms of prejudice: (a) perceiving women less favorably than men as potential occupants of leadership roles and (b) evaluating behavior that fulfills the prescriptions of a leader role less favorably when it is enacted by a woman" ([34], p. 575). It is evident that these prejudices, whether conscious or unconscious, create double binds for women with preparedness to become leaders and create double standards. If the paradigm persists that women can only be communal versus agentic leaders, there will be slow progress for change in institutions that purport to want to advance women into senior administrative positions.

Emotional Intelligence and Resonant Leadership

Emotional intelligence (EI) is often referred to as a qualitative approach to understanding and relating to people, requiring leaders to know themselves to better engage with direct reports, peers, and superiors alike [42, 43]. The four components of the EI model are self-awareness, self-management, social awareness, and relationship management. Embedded in the model is emotional self-management based on the premise that leaders need to be aware of why their emotions are triggered and how to regulate them at the moment. The EI model has been compared to the multicultural counseling competency (MCC) paradigm with interacting domains of awareness, knowledge, and skills/behaviors [70]. Although the MCC was developed for application in counseling settings, it has broad applicability for work settings for employees and leaders alike, as discussed in the multicultural organizational development section of this chapter. For example, MCC awareness and knowledge can lead to greater perspective-taking and empathy. In an academic department, leaders must be conscious of their tendency to have all faculty fit the same mold when it comes to teaching style, participation in meetings, and "productivity." Through perspective-taking, leaders may recognize that female professors have more responsibilities for student advising than their male colleagues that may interfere in their research hours.

In a qualitative study of Latina women administrators [3], the theme of resonant leadership emerged. In practice, resonant leadership means people engage through their values and "can prolong the positive emotions they arouse through their encouraging and attentive behavior" [78]. Resonant leadership also indicates the capacity to demonstrate empathy and understanding. Dissonant leadership typically provokes emotionally dissonant behavior because of the leader's less relational and affirming behaviors.

Further examples from the Latina leaders study point to the way women negotiate problematic situations for themselves and others. One associate provost encountered hostility from her new direct reports, and the male whom everyone thought should have been appointed although he did not possess a doctoral degree. His posture was passive-aggressive, coaching her to speak up less because her predecessor had been a quiet woman. Rather than ignore his suggestion, she invited him to meet and explore how he could be an asset to her in her new role. She also asked what new responsibilities he might want to take on since he had considerable experiences in the provost's office. This expression of inclusion and empathy on her part was met favorably and gave her more latitude to assert herself with others who harbored negative feelings toward her. Through this visible alignment, she also demonstrated agentic leadership of courage and independence.

Another example of resonant leadership by women of color in STEM is addressed in a text with contributions by women from different Historically Black Colleges and Universities (HBCU) [36]. These women were part of an academic leadership program called OURS for STEM faculty that provided a paradigm of awareness, knowledge, and skill-building to advance in their professions and institutions. The book has two major sections. The first gives voice to African American women's career journeys as they navigated the academy with both tribulations and celebrations. They described the identity career challenges as young women scientists at an HBCU, where leadership was primarily male. Moreover, they experienced minimization and microaggressions because of their female identity. The second part of the book speaks to leadership opportunities sought and achieved and the challenges of being an agent of change as a woman of color. A few examples of change were creating a promotion and tenure handbook for the institution, establishing cross-disciplinary/departmental working groups to benefit students' retention in the sciences and the university overall, and forging university-community partnerships, particularly with local businesses. In all of these examples, the women had to step out of their regular assignments and role, broaden her given faculty role, and initiate needed change. Through the leadership program, they had learned about the art of proposing ideas, negotiating time and space to advance these, and using their voice.

In all situations, the women advocated for the benefit of students, the program, the university, and other stakeholders. In the process, they gained greater affirmation of their competence and capabilities.

Summary

Feminist models and feminist psychology have been the centerpieces of this chapter. The discussion points to the continuous efforts of women to advance women's knowledge, worldviews, interpersonal strengths, lived experiences, and intersecting identities as assets in different contexts, including higher education. The sociohistorical and sociocultural conditions in the USA provide essential context about why it has been and continues to be a challenge for women to advance professionally. As discussed in this chapter, women of diverse backgrounds have had to carve out their niche, their position, and their raison d'etre. Feminism and the psychology of women provide worldviews that advance the essentiality of diversity, access, equity, and inclusion. The diversity and intersectionality of women are always present in workspaces and social settings. Our identities are complex and not limited to one check-off box on an intake form. With each additional dimension of identity because of a degree earned, a new position, or a workplace promotion, a woman further differentiates herself, disrupting the status quo that wants to define women. However, systems of socialization that delimit and marginalize women, and send messages about deficiencies, upset a woman's sense of self-esteem and self-efficacy. Sadly, these messages can come from a woman's family, work setting, and trusted friends. This statement forecasts the following chapter that examines organizational workplace cultures, particularly in the academy. The culture of the academy for women has not been one of welcoming and inclusion. Thus, recognizing the "borderlands" women have to navigate in STEM will deepen the discussion about how women continue to transcend unwelcoming and chilly workplaces.

References

1. Anand, T. (2018, April 26). *A brief summary of the third wave of feminism*. Feminism In India. https://feminisminindia.com/2018/04/27/brief-summary-third-wave-of-feminism/
2. Arredondo, P. (2011). The "borderlands" experience for women of color as higher education leaders. In J. L. Martin (Ed.), *Women as leaders in education: Succeeding despite inequity, discrimination, and other challenges* (pp. 275–298). Santa Barbara: Praeger Press.
3. Arredondo, P. (2018). Latinx women aspiring, persisting, and maintaining cultural integrity. In P. A. Perez (Ed.), *The tenure-track process for Chicana and Latina Faculty: Experiences of resisting and persisting in the academy* (pp. 106–129). London: Taylor & Francis.
4. Arredondo, P., & Glauner, T. (1992). *Personal dimensions of identity model*. Empowerment Workshops, Inc.
5. Arredondo, P., Psalti, A., & Celia, K. (1993). The woman factor in multicultural counseling. *Counseling and Human Development, 25*(8), 1–8.

6. Arredondo, P., Toporek, R., Brown, S. P., Jones, J., Locke, D. C., Sanchez, J., & Stadler, H. (1996). Operationalization of the multicultural counseling competencies. *Journal of Multicultural Counseling and Development, 24*(1), 42–78. https://doi.org/10.1002/j.2161-1912.1996.tb00288.x.

7. Beal, F. (n.d.). *Double Jeopardy: To Be Black & Female*. Radical Education Project.

8. Beauvoir, S. de. (1949). *Le deuxième sexe*. Gallimard.

9. Beauvoir, S. de, Borde, C., & Malovany-Chevallier, S. (2009). *The second sex*. Knopf Doubleday Publishing Group. http://banq.lib.overdrive.com/ContentDetails.htm?id=00038A93-7B24-4653-94E6-9C4689DA09EA

10. Belenky, M. F., Clinchy, B. M., Goldberger, N., & Tarule, J. M. (Eds.). (1986). *Women's ways of knowing: The development of self, voice, and mind* (10th anniversary ed). BasicBooks.

11. Bell, A. E., Spencer, S. J., Iserman, E., & Logel, C. E. R. (2003). Stereotype threat and women's performance in engineering. *Journal of Engineering Education, 92*(4), 307–312. https://doi.org/10.1002/j.2168-9830.2003.tb00774.x.

12. Block, C., Cruz, M., Bairley, M., Harel-Marian, T., & Roberson, L. (2018). Inside the prism of an invisible threat: Shining a light on the hidden work of contending with systemic stereotype threat in STEM fields. *Journal of Vocational Behavior.* https://doi.org/10.1016/j.jvb.2018.09.007.

13. Borland, E. (2020, May 13). *Standpoint theory*. Encyclopedia Britannica. https://www.britannica.com/topic/standpoint-theory

14. Bravata, D. M., Watts, S. A., Keefer, A. L., Madhusudhan, D. K., Taylor, K. T., Clark, D. M., Nelson, R. S., Cokley, K. O., & Hagg, H. K. (2020). Prevalence, Predictors, and Treatment of Impostor Syndrome: A Systematic Review. *Journal of General Internal Medicine, 35*(4), 1252–1275. https://doi.org/10.1007/s11606-019-05364-1.

15. Burkett, E. (2020, March 5). *Women's rights movement*. Encyclopedia Britannica. https://www.britannica.com/event/womens-movement

16. Burkett, E., & Burnell, L. (2020, March 6). *Feminism—The second wave of feminism*. Encyclopædia Britannica, Inc. https://www.britannica.com/topic/feminism/The-second-wave-of-feminism

17. Canning, E. A., LaCosse, J., Kroeper, K. M., & Murphy, M. (2019). Feeling like an imposter: The effect of perceived classroom competition on the daily psychological experiences of first-generation college students – Elizabeth A. Canning, Jennifer LaCosse, Kathryn M. Kroeper, Mary C. Murphy, 2020. *Social Psychological and Personality Science, 11*(5), 647–657.

18. Carli, L. L., & Eagly, A. H. (2016). Women face a labyrinth: An examination of metaphors for women leaders. *Gender in Management: An International Journal, 31*(8), 514–527. https://doi.org/10.1108/GM-02-2015-0007.

19. Cherry, K. (2020, March 28). *Why Karen Horney Is Important to Feminine Psychology*. Verywell Mind. https://www.verywellmind.com/karen-horney-biography-2795539

20. Chiwaya, N. (2018, October 11). *New data on #MeToo's first year shows "undeniable" impact.* NBC News. https://www.nbcnews.com/news/us-news/new-data-metoo-s-first-year-shows-undeniable-impact-n918821

21. Churchill, L. B. (2020, February 19). *The Feminine Mystique*. Encyclopædia Britannica, Inc. https://www.britannica.com/topic/The-Feminine-Mystique

22. Collins, P. H. (1990). *Black feminist thought: Knowledge, consciousness, and the politics of empowerment*. London: Taylor & Francis.

23. Comas-Díaz, L., & Bryant-Davis, T. (2016). *Womanist and Mujerista psychologies: Voices of fire, acts of courage*. Washington, DC: American Psychological Association.

24. Comas-Díaz, L., & Greene, B. (2013). *Psychological health of women of color: Intersections, challenges, and opportunities*.

25. Comas-Diaz, L., & Vazquez, C. I. (2018). *The practice of Latina psychologists: Thriving in the cultural borderlands*. London: Taylor & Francis/Routledge.

26. Conarton, S., & Kreger Silverman, L. (1988). Feminine development through the life cycle. In M. A. Dutton & L. E. Walker (Eds.), *Feminist psychotherapies: Integration of therapeutic and feminist systems* (pp. 37–63). Ablex Publishing Corporation.
27. Cooney, S. (2018, November 19). *Here are some of the women who made history in the midterm elections.* Time. https://time.com/5323592/2018-elections-women-history-records/
28. Crenshaw, K. (*1989*). Demarginalizing the intersection of race and sex: A black feminist critique of antidiscrimination doctrine, feminist theory and antiracist politics. *University of Chicago Legal Forum, 1989*(1), 31.
29. Denmark, F. L., & Paludi, M. A. (Eds.). (2018). *Women and Leadership.* Springer International Publishing. https://doi.org/10.1007/978-3-319-72182-8.
30. Denmark, F., & Paludi, M. A. (2007). *Psychology of women: Handbook of issues and theories.* Greenwood Publishing Group.
31. Dutton-Douglas, M. A., & Walker, L. E. (1988). *Feminine development through the life cycle.* Ablex Publishing Corporation.
32. Eagly, A. H., & Chin, J. L. (2010). Diversity and leadership in a changing world. *American Psychologist, 65*(3), 216–224. https://doi.org/10.1037/a0018957.
33. Eagly, A. H., & Karau, S. J. (1991). Gender and the emergence of leaders: A meta-analysis. *Journal of Personality and Social Psychology, 60*(5), 685–710. https://doi.org/10.1037/0022-3514.60.5.685.
34. Eagly, A. H., & Karau, S. J. (2002). Role congruity theory of prejudice toward female leaders. *Psychological Review, 109*(3), 573. https://doi.org/10.1037/0033-295X.109.3.573.
35. Else-Quest, N. M., & Hyde, J. S. (2020). *The psychology of women and gender* (9th ed.). SAGE. https://us.sagepub.com/en-us/nam/the-psychology-of-women-and-gender/book256936
36. Engerman, K., Luster-Teasley, S., Washington, C., & Bolden-Tiller, O. (2016). *Women called to lead: Empowering women of color in academic leadership.* Santa Barbara: Fielding Graduate University.
37. Enns, C. Z., Williams, E. N., & Fassinger, R. E. (2012, September 19). Feminist multicultural psychology: Evolution, change, and challenge. In *The Oxford handbook of feminist multicultural counseling psychology.* Oxford: Oxford University Press. https://doi.org/10.1093/oxfordhb/9780199744220.013.0001.
38. Fazackerley, A. (2020, May 12). Women's research plummets during lockdown—But articles from men increase | Higher education | The Guardian. *The Guardian.* https://www.theguardian.com/education/2020/may/12/womens-research-plummets-during-lockdown-but-articles-from-men-increase
39. Fiske, S. T. (1993). Controlling other people: The impact of power on stereotyping. *American Psychologist, 48*(6), 621. https://doi.org/10.1037/0003-066X.48.6.621.
40. Friedan, B. (1964). *Feminine mystique.* Norton. https://www.thriftbooks.com/w/the-feminine-mystique_betty-friedan/246520/
41. Gilligan, C. (1982). *In A Different Voice: Psychological Theory and Women's Development* (Vol. 326). Harvard University Press.
42. Goleman, D. (1995). *Emotional intelligence: why it can matter more than IQ.* Random House Publishing Group.
43. Goleman, D., Boyatzis, R. E., & McKee, A. (2002). *Primal leadership: Realizing the power of emotional intelligence.* Harvard Business School Press.
44. Greene, B. (1994). Ethnic-minority lesbians and gay men: Mental health and treatment issues. *Journal of Consulting and Clinical Psychology, 62*(2), 243–251. https://doi.org/10.1037//0022-006x.62.2.243.
45. Hannah, S. T. (2006). Agentic leadership efficacy: Test of a new construct and model for development and performance. *The University of Nebraska – Lincoln, ProQuest Dissertations Publishing.* https://digitalcommons.unl.edu/dissertations/AAI3208108
46. HANX Official. (2019). *The 15 most famous feminists throughout history.* HANX. https://www.hanxofficial.com/blogs/naked-truths/the-15-most-famous-feminists-throughout-history
47. Harding, S. G. (1986). *The science question in feminism.* Cornell University Press.

48. Harding, S. G. (2004). *The feminist standpoint theory reader: Intellectual and political controversies.* Psychology Press.
49. Helms, J. E. (1990). Toward a model of white racial identity development. In J. E. Helms (Ed.), *Black and White racial identity: Theory, research, and practice.* Greenwood Publishing Group.
50. Hersey, P., Blanchard, K. H., & Johnson, D. E. (2008). *Management of Organizational Behavior: Leading Human Resources.* Pearson Prentice Hall.
51. bell hooks (1981). *Ain't I a woman: Black women and feminism.* South End Press.
52. bell hooks (1984). *Feminist theory from margin to center.* South End Press.
53. Horney, K. (1937). *The collected works of Karen Horney.* Norton.
54. Horney, K. (1967). *Feminine psychology.* W. W. Norton & Company.
55. Jamieson, J. P., & Harkins, S. G. (2007). Mere effort and stereotype threat performance effects. *Journal of Personality and Social Psychology, 93*(4), 544–564. https://doi.org/10.1037/0022-3514.93.4.544.
56. Johnson, V. J. (1997). Weavers of change. *Dissertation Abstracts International, 59*(1), 36A. https://doi.org/10.25335/M5T14TT02.
57. Jordan, J. V., Kaplan, A. G., Miller, J. B., Stiver, I. P., & Surrey, J. L. (1991). *Women's growth in connection: Writings from the Stone Center.* Guilford Publications.
58. McClelland, D. C. (1975). *Power: The inner experience.* Irvington Publishers.
59. McGregor, D. (1960). *The human side of enterprise.* McGraw-Hill.
60. Miller, J. B. (1976). *Toward a new psychology of women* (pp. xi, 143). Beacon.
61. Millett, K. (1970). *Sexual politics.* Columbia University Press.
62. Minthorn, R., & Chavez, A. F. (2014). *Indigenous leadership in higher education.* London: Taylor & Francis.
63. Pennington, C. R., Heim, D., Levy, A. R., & Larkin, D. T. (2016). Twenty years of stereotype threat research: A review of psychological mediators. *PLoS ONE, 11*(1). https://doi.org/10.1371/journal.pone.0146487.
64. Rosette, A. S., & Tost, L. P. (2010). Agentic women and communal leadership: How role prescriptions confer advantage to top women leaders. *Journal of Applied Psychology, 95*(2), 221–235. https://doi.org/10.1037/a0018204.
65. Sanford, L. T., & Donovan, M. E. (1984). *Women and self-esteem.* Penguin Books.
66. Smith, D. E. (1987). *The everyday world as problematic: A feminist sociology.* NorthEastern University Press.
67. Steele, C. M., & Aronson, J. (1995). Stereotype threat and the intellectual test performance of African Americans. *Journal of Personality and Social Psychology, 69*(5), 797–811. https://doi.org/10.1037/0022-3514.69.5.797.
68. Steinmetz, K. (2020, February 20). She coined the term 'Intersectionality' over 30 years ago. Here's what it means to her today. *Time.* https://time.com/5786710/kimberle-crenshaw-intersectionality/
69. Stupak, V. C., & Stupak, R. J. (1990). Carl Jung, feminism, and modern structural realities. *International Review of Modern Sociology, 20*(2), 267–276. JSTOR.
70. Sue, D. W., Arredondo, P., & McDavis, R. J. (1992). Multicultural counseling competencies and standards: A call to the profession. *Journal of Multicultural Counseling and Development, 20*(2), 64–88. https://doi.org/10.1002/j.2161-1912.1992.tb00563.x.
71. Tannen, D. (1990). Gender differences in conversational coherence: Physical alignment and topical cohesion. In *Conversational organization and its development* (pp. 167–206). Ablex Publishing.
72. Tao, K. W., & Gloria, A. M. (2018). Should I Stay or Should I Go? The Role of Impostorism in STEM Persistence. *Psychology of Women Quarterly, 43*(2), 151–164. https://doi.org/10.1177/0361684318802333.
73. The Editors of Encyclopaedia Britannica. (2019, December 2). *Karen Horney | German psychoanalyst.* Encyclopedia Britannica. https://www.britannica.com/biography/Karen-Horney
74. The Trustees of Columbia University in the City of New York. (2017, June 8). *Kimberlé Crenshaw on intersectionality, more than two decades later.* Columbia Law School. https://

www.law.columbia.edu/news/archive/kimberle-crenshaw-intersectionality-more-two-decades-later

75. Travis, C. B., White, J. W., Rutherford, A., Williams, W. S., Cook, S. L., & Wyche, K. F. (Eds.). (2018). *APA handbook of the psychology of women: History, theory, and battlegrounds,* (Vol. 1, pp. xxii, 632). American Psychological Association. doi:https://doi.org/10.1037/0000059-000

76. Wollstonecraft, M. (1796). *A vindication of the rights of woman: With strictures on political and moral subjects.* J. Johnson.

77. Women's Studies. (2016, September 5). Gradschools. https://www.gradschools.com/programs/womens-studies

78. Arredondo, P. (2019). Latinx women aspiring, persisting, and maintaining cultural integrity. In: P. Perez (Ed.), *In their own words: Chicana and Latina Faculty Resisting and Persisting in the Academy,* 106–129.

Chapter 3
Organizational Culture and Climate: Historic Systemic Barriers for Women

Introduction

In her work on diversity management strategies in organizations, Arredondo [4] asserted that organizational culture is fluid and not static. Culture evolves. Her premise was that the culture of organizations is subject to change because of the multiple contextual factors that influence and the inputs of individuals who are part of the organization. Culture is a term derived principally from anthropologists' work with reference to how cultures, generally non-Western, were organized structurally, functionally, and relationally. Kluckhohn and Kroeber [38] cataloged more than 100 definitions and emerged with a comprehensive statement:

> *Culture represents patterns, explicit and implicit, of and for behavior acquired and transmitted by symbols, constituting the distinctive achievement of human groups, including their embodiment in artifacts; the essential core of culture consists of traditional (i.e., historically derived and selected) ideas and especially their attached values; culture systems may, on the one hand, be considered as products of action, on the other, as conditioning elements of future action* ([38], p. 181).

Corporations, hospitals, banks, governmental agencies and universities are organizations with macro-cultures. Within a university and all other entities mentioned are the microcultures represented by internal- and external-facing departments, all integral to the operations and functioning. Hospitals have departments with different specialties and a workforce comprised of medical specialists to service staff. Consumer goods businesses like Walmart and Target have departments for human resources, marketing, finance, and customer service. Then there are universities in the business of education with academic departments and centers and student-serving units, particularly Student Affairs. Now, most organizations also have the Office of the Chief Diversity Officer, charged with a systemic strategy for diversity, equity, and inclusion. All microunits in these organizations have a unique culture per the

P. Arredondo et al., *Women and the Challenge of STEM Professions*, International and Cultural Psychology, https://doi.org/10.1007/978-3-030-62201-5_3

definition by Kroeber and Kluckhohn. Still, because they are part of a system, they also share the established macro values, norms, traditions, language, and structures.

In this chapter, the organizational or institutional culture will be discussed broadly, insomuch as the main theories about organizations still describe highly structured, hierarchical, male-created entities. We will also draw upon the research of anthropologists, psychologists, and sociologists to examine processes and mindsets that influence organizations to hold on to their prevailing cultures. Of course, with attention to women in STEM in this book, there will be a discussion of women's presence in higher learning institutions and other work environments. As one example, the labyrinth (A. [17]) is one of the metaphors to describe how women navigate organizations not designed for them. In STEM doctoral programs and academic units, women are often still considered outsiders, to a point regularly made to feel unwelcome. In these male-designed systems and structures, issues of climate, role expectancy, power, and privilege manifest and disadvantage women. The qualitative experiences of women as outsiders will be discussed by examining terms such as tokenism, marginalization, microaggressions, and so forth. These experiences of exclusion, minimization, ridicule, and so forth often cause women to leave positions they are well-qualified to hold. Finally, theories of women's leadership and how these apply to STEM women in the academy will be examined.

Cultural Variations Across Organizations

"All organizations and institutions have a culture" ([4], p. 8). This culture begins with a history, philosophy, and mission established by the founders. The bank JPMorgan Chase, initially founded by Aaron Burr and J.P. Morgan in 1799, for example, has had many iterations due to mergers and acquisitions, changes in regulations, global finance, and so forth. A financial institution serves its shareholders; thus, revenues are a priority for the shareholders, not customers. Alternatively, Catalyst is a nonprofit organization established in 1962 with the purpose of partnering with employers to support women's career development trajectory. Subsequently, Catalyst has become a leader in research about women's opportunities or lack thereof, primarily in the corporate sector. The term "glass ceiling" was given more attention through their research, although the metaphor is said to have first emerged in 1986 [34]. The term signals the artificial barriers and unwritten rules to women's advancement because of conditions of inequality and male-centered cultures. The latter included pay inequities, gender discrimination and sexual harassment without remediation, and male norms for success. The term also came into the discussion with the presidential candidate Hillary Clinton who faced the challenges of stepping into the role typically reserved for men. The "glass ceiling" metaphor is also applied to persons of color or individuals from LGBTQ and disability status who are often viewed through deficit lenses in all institutions, and not "good fits" for leadership roles, including in universities.

Though university culture will be discussed further in the next section, two examples will be mentioned herein. Boston College (BC) is a Jesuit Catholic university, established in 1863 in response to the growing Irish immigrant population in Greater Boston and a statement of self-determination. At the time, men of Catholic heritage were not admitted to Harvard University, across the river [23]. Smith College remains today a private women's liberal arts college, located in Northampton, Massachusetts. Its slogan is "In Virtue (One Gains) Knowledge" in contrast to the BC slogan of "Ever to Excel." These brief descriptions show that all of these institutions have a purpose, values, and practices that communicate an identity to individuals of diverse backgrounds that may or may not be seen as approachable, desirable, or culturally resonant.

The history and cultural ethos of organizations also signal their track record of outright exclusion through discriminatory policies and practices and, alternatively, the inclusion of women, persons of color, and other underrepresented groups. In higher education, it is not just the sciences, engineering, and medicine that have proven unwelcome to women students and professionals but also the vast majority of workplaces. The founders of an organization and its contemporary leadership signal their consciousness about diversity, equity, inclusion, and access.

Situating Women in the Workplace

For whom were contemporary workplaces designed? The easy response is "men." From anthropologists' accountings, tribal societies distributed men and women's work with an external and internal focus on strength and women's childbearing role [2]. Gender role expectations relegated men to outdoor agricultural work, hunting, and warfare, and women to tending the home and the children. Men set the rules as well.

In the "Cult of True Womanhood" or the "Cult of Domesticity," Barbara Welter [54] describes the prevailing expectations for women in the UK and the USA from 1820 through 1860. She described the attributes of womanhood as centering on piety, purity, submissiveness, and domesticity. By complying with these virtues, Welter asserted that women believed they would have power, be liked, and be successful. The messages about where women belonged were clear—not in public workspaces. However, for women of color, women immigrants, and poor White women of a lower socioeconomic class, the invisibility and oppression leading to submissiveness was intentional. Black women brought up the children of the masters, poor White women from Ireland were the cleaning ladies of affluent families, and Latinas were in the fields, picking crops and exposed to pesticides that poisoned their being.

Stratification of women in organizations continues based on ethnicity/race, education, and other social determinants that create pay inequities. In hospital settings, it is predominantly White men in charge as administrators and physicians, women as nurses, and a few more in the administrative and physician roles. More often than not, the majority of women of color are aides, food servers, and cleaning staff. Universities are also stratified with the academic and administrators, once again, primarily White men, being in roles of leadership. Stratification promotes workplace classism and, in many instances, keeps the glass ceiling in place.

Organizations also have cultural norms and practices that do not necessarily support women balancing work and family priorities. In many organizations, including universities, references are often made to the "mommy track," indicating that women cannot meet the rigor of promotion and tenure at the specified time because of mothering responsibilities. A 2012 survey by the Coalition on the Academic Workforce puts the number of female adjuncts even higher, at nearly 62% [9]. Among some of the more historically cliched statements are that "women's work is in the home," that homemaking and childcare are the woman's domain, and that men are the primary breadwinners. These are old assumptions that continue to color the expectations about women professionals, women who are scientists, faculty, and mothers. Women adjuncts are talented women with doctorates. Many leave the tenure-track ranks because of childcare responsibilities. Unlike men, women do not have the stereotypical wife at home to manage the home and children.

Women in the World of Work: 2021

Due to social norms, it is believed that before being a career woman, a woman's primary role is becoming a wife and mother. Of course, in 2021, traditional roles for women have been modified and evolved influenced by feminist worldviews, economic necessities, and the mere fact that women have changed. Federal data indicate that as of December 2019, women comprised 50.4% of the workforce [32]. For the past decade, the percentage of women in the labor force has not gone below 49%. There are expectations that steady increases will continue as there are more women single heads of household, college-educated, and working in fields of healthcare, education, and the service industry. The latter labor fields have been primarily composed of women and women of color, immigrant women, and single mothers. Women in traditionally male fields have also increased. This is notable in law enforcement, firefighters, construction, and the professions of law, medicine, and the sciences.

One of three lawyers are women [14], yet men continue to be higher earners. Inequity in salaries is based on two facts: (1) Women assuming professional work are younger, and (2) starting salaries are inequitable, leading to low earning for women. Data for women in medicine are reported in categories of academic medicine, practicing physicians, and so forth. One figure that jumped out was that women from underrepresented groups in academic medicine stood at 12% in 2009 and merely 13% in 2018 [1]. As for women in the science professions—physical sciences, engineering, and medicine—the National Academy provides different types of reporting based on particular fields as well as the context. Generally, it is easier to point to data on women in academic, medical, and university engineering and science departments. The percentages are small.

2021 Roles and Identity Congruence

As more women engage in the work world outside of the home and are forming careers, they have more frequent potential to experience multiple-role engagement. Attributions about women who assume multiple responsibilities have often led to "othering" expressions or demeaning and trivial labels. When women assume work that is traditionally seen as men's work, they are accused of taking away a man's employment. Women who step into administrative leadership roles are often held to a higher standard and scrutinized to a greater degree than their male counterparts [35]. Kanter's book was an opening to the examination and exposure of double standards for women, particularly in corporate settings. She had a follow-up video that addressed the "O" factor in organizations. The "O" can be the other or the outsider, generally the person who integrates a department or office; this could be a woman, person of color, LGBTQ self-identified individual, or someone with disability status. The "O" is highly visible because of her difference, and thus, she is expected to provide the "O" viewpoint, be exemplary or twice as good, and conform to the rules. The "O," according to Kanter, is highly scrutinized because of her difference. It can be fairly stated that there are many more "O"s in universities today, including STEM women. Thus, this concept remains relevant to examine the context of DEI initiatives underway in universities.

Sumra and Schillaci [50] conducted a study to gain insight into whether women who engage in multiple social roles experience more or less stress than women in fewer roles. Researchers gathered data regarding perceptions of stress, social capital, and life satisfaction based on social demographics, including income, age group, education, and hours of employment. A nonrandom sample of 308 women in North America over the age of 18 participated in the study. Survey results and multiple regression statistical analysis provided evidence that multiple-role engagement was not associated with significantly higher life stress or reduced life satisfaction. Participants reported participating in an average of 2.86 roles from a list of 7 roles, having an average network size of 17.38 individuals, and an average life satisfaction score of 2.52, indicating moderate to high life satisfaction. Implications of this finding point to the need to examine the nature of the intensity of specific roles and related stress conditions, and the stress response known as "tending and befriending" thought to be exercised by women during perceived threats to well-being.

The term "Superwoman Syndrome" has been used to describe the stressful experience of women who strive to "do it all." The superwoman is viewed as an identity archetype, referring to a woman who performs multiple, concurrent full-time roles. Role theory presents opposing perspectives explaining the effects of assuming multiple roles on stress applying two hypotheses. The depletion hypothesis indicates that an increased number of roles leads to overload and strain or burnout. The enrichment hypothesis focuses on multiple-role engagement, "enhancing an individual's resources, social connections, power, prestige, and emotional gratification" [50]. Perhaps it is time to revisit the superwoman syndrome attribution since contemporary professional women are more insightful about the self-limitations needed in their personal and work lives. However, work and family balance challenges remain. Further, in 2021, the concept seems more stigmatizing than explanatory about the complexity of women's lives and our multiple identities.

Academic Culture and Climate

Culture and climate are attributes of all organizations, as has been discussed thus far. But in higher education, the culture of heteropatriarchy, heterosexism, whiteness, socioeconomic privilege, and elitism has to be recognized. What is also important to acknowledge is the university culture and how this has historical and politically established structures, processes, and practices for exclusion and inclusion, thereby perpetuating sameness. In "The University Culture," Simplicio [47] outlines how an institution's history, values, and traditions define its culture, and the role of gatekeepers, particularly tenured faculty, to keep history alive. As discussed, these gatekeepers also include staff members with longevity and seniority. Together, the senior faculty and staff often set the boundaries for complex relationships, empowering themselves to maintain the status quo. With this scenario in place, it is apparent how challenging it would be for women or persons from an underrepresented group to wedge into this university culture of self-preservation.

Another perspective is that the academic culture defines the university culture and campus culture. The latter manifests through individualism, academic ethics, scientific research, academic norms and regulations, creativity, and leadership [46]. As such, the authors state that there is a symbiosis between campus and academic culture, with the latter enhancing the former. Alternatively, they indicate that campus culture can condition and restrict academic culture by straying away from the academic mission and not supporting the academic space's evolution and innovation. Evidence or examples include the anti-war and lowering the voting age amid the Vietnam War. The national movements led to activism on college campuses and responses from the college administration. Some of the responses included policy changes for universities to be more inclusive of students' voices and "demands."

In the last 5 years, there has been activism related to free speech and the Black Lives Matter movement. These major sociopolitical and sociocultural movements are interventions that upset the status quo as students, faculty, and staff alike assert their rights to participatory governance. The COVID-19 pandemic and racial unrest of 2020–2021 are other examples of significant disruptions in the university modus operandi. There is no certainty as of this writing about how campus culture and structures will change and what university structures and practices will persist. There are many unknowns in the midst of a changing demographic map in the USA.

Concepts and Theories Relevant for Academic Culture

Cultural dimensions in the workplace are reference points for recognizing how assumptions and attributes about communication behavior occur. Hall [24, 25], an anthropologist, described how low and high context or the environment influences communication patterns and practices. In high context cultures such as Japan, Greece, and Saudi Arabia, communication tends to be more nonverbal and situational, and individuals rely on previous or established relationships to convey a message. Because of the nonverbal tendencies, body language matters as does the status and titles of the individuals. With high context communication, there are unstated expectations and more implicit understanding. In low context cultures, there is more verbal communication with stated expectations and written documentation and specific agreements. Low context countries include England, Germany, Switzerland, and the USA. Thus, in US workplaces, there are more verbal exchanges, documentation of meetings, and stated expectations. In theory, this seems reasonable, but institutional cultures will also set the tone for the types of communication exchanges that are most desirable and how these exchanges occur—verbal, written, group, or via teams.

Research by sociolinguist Debra Tannen about communication biases as these affect women are captured in her famous text, *You Just Don't Understand* (1990). She emphasized that men and women seek different outcomes through conversations, particularly independence versus intimacy. This can lead to exchanges that are often at cross-purposes.

> *For most women, the language of conversation is primarily a language of rapport: a way of establishing connections and negotiating relationships ... For most men, talk is primarily a means to preserve independence and negotiate and maintain status in a hierarchical social order.* ([51], p. 77)

This quote illuminates the patterns of communication typical in universities with layers of structures and hierarchies. Tannen points out that men typically dominate conversations. In department meetings, men often interrupt, talk over others, and otherwise try to command the discussions. Women's early socialization to remain quiet or silent may come into play in these settings, rendering voiceless, or when they speak up, a man may readily interrupt, take her idea, and move the discussion in another direction. With ingrained communication patterns in academic units, newcomers, particularly junior professors of color, and women in general, will not easily be heard or invited to speak by their senior male colleagues. Exclusionary communication practices are another example of the chilly climate in higher education.

The Chilly Climate in Higher Education

The history of STEM women in the academy begins long before they earn doctorates or become professors. Discouraging girls from studying math and science has been long-standing with immediate implications for career paths never taken. For those who do choose STEM undergraduate studies, the experiences can be harrowing. The environmental factors affecting women have been described as the "chilly climate," a term attributed to Bernice Sandler (1982). The "chilly climate" describes the subtle and not subtle ways men and women are treated differently in the classroom and at work [26]. Through a series of interviews and reviews of the literature on the experiences of women students and professionals in universities, Hall and Sandler found [26] a number of behaviors they termed "microinequities" that in most situations adversely affected women's opportunities and experiences. Among these were lower expectations, presumed incompetence, exclusion, discouragement, and overt hostile behavior. For example, they found that male students are more often called upon than female students and selected to be professors' research assistants. In research meetings, women doctoral students were questioned about their seriousness for the research they hoped to conduct. The sexist language was also used when addressing women, including "honey," "dear," and "sweetie." Women and persons of color were often singled out for their opinion on behalf of their "presumed" identity group affiliation.

In an updated article, Sandler [45] indicated the references to women were all-inclusive. However, she acknowledged that the conditions for women of color, women with disabilities, lesbians, and older women were probably treated differently because of their difference. She also noted that the chilly climate likely also affected men of color, individuals who spoke English as a second language, and working-class backgrounds. She referred to them as "outsiders" in the higher education space. Hall and Sandler [26, 27] were particularly taken with the work environment for students and faculty in the sciences. In mixed classes and labs, women were often relegated to be the assistant of male students and tasked to take notes in a faculty meeting. In short, how a classroom feels and how one's colleagues behave will affect women's desire to stay or leave.

In studies with undergraduate women, primarily White, researchers found differences in perceptions about the chilly climate. The research found an increased cynicism and emotional exhaustion though not lower academic efficacy [33]. There were constant challenges. Jensen commented that the "woman – scientist identity interference" she referred to in her study [33] describes the incongruence felt about being a woman and a scientist. Experiences for women of color and transgender women were not explicitly addressed in the study.

Ironically, in subsequent studies about women's experiences in the chilly climate [10], women scientists reject the notion that gender plays a role in the workplace or their experiences. In her study with 102 women, she found that they often resist the term "chilly climate" to describe their work environment and deny that there is inequality based on gender. However, there is evidence to the contrary [10].

Organizational Theories and Their Application in Contemporary Institutions

Research by Hofstede [7, 30, 31] is relevant in discussions of organizational culture and the biases introduced in its structures, processes, and leadership. A Dutch social psychologist, Hofstede, conducted a global research study of national cultural values across 50 countries when working with IBM in the 1950s. His findings yielded an index on five cultural dimensions. These are individualism versus collectivism, femininity versus masculinity, power distance (low to high), uncertainty avoidance (high to low on the index), and long- versus short-term orientation. His premise is that a cultural mindset is influenced by socialization in one's country of origin and reinforced or challenged in organizations and communities [7]. The findings across the 50 countries surveyed revealed that biases toward masculinity were more pronounced in countries where male roles were elevated and sanctified and those of women were of second-class status. This was reported for most Middle East and Latin American countries. Femininity scores were more elevated in Scandinavian countries and Canada and recognized for their pluralistic attitudes toward childcare and other assigned roles usually left for women. Although the USA has anti-discrimination laws in place that apply in workplaces, the glass ceiling continues to limit women's access and opportunities to top administrative positions. The organizational culture of universities still seems to favor men based on the small number of women university presidents and an even lower number for women of color and other underrepresented groups. Also notable is that the boards of trustees or boards of directors are primarily White men. These are the individuals who make decisions about the appointment of senior administrators. Considering intersectionality in this discussion, one may readily note that men have dimensions of identity that are most often seen as signs of leadership and authority, power, and privilege. White males with degrees in business from a prestigious university will likely be selected for a CEO or presidency position over a woman with a degree in psychology from a woman's university.

When applying Hofstede's index in contemporary higher education, it is possible to spotlight the values for individualism, high power distance (full professors to junior professors), and masculinity based merely on the predominant presence of men in tenured positions, as deans and provosts, etc. The opportunities for women to enter the academy and to remain in the academy are complex. It is often argued that STEM faculty prefer to hire more qualified women over equally qualified men. However, audits of hiring practices report that women are not selected when they are in a pool against more accomplished men [13]. Though women and men may have the same credentials, men are those hired.

Women in the professoriate are a growing sector of the academy, but most are not on the tenure track. Among adjunct professors, the majority are women and persons of color, primarily women of color [20]. Underrepresented minority groups held approximately 13% of faculty jobs in 2013, up from 9% in 1993. Yet they still only hold 10% of tenured jobs, according to the study. Women now hold 49% of total faculty positions but only 38% of tenured jobs [19]. These research findings tend to support Hofstede's indexes of masculinity versus femininity and how these engrained mindsets from national culture are transmitted into organizational cultures.

Multicultural Organizational Development

Diversity, equity, inclusion, and access (DEIA) are themes in contemporary organizations, meant to signal values and practices for fairness, respect, and possibilities. Many organizations and universities in the year 2020 have engaged consultants to support their initiatives for more inclusive hiring practices, programs for retention of underrepresented employees, and cultural competency education. However, diversity initiatives are about change and, as such, can upset the power and politics of the organization. A chemistry department that hires a woman as department chair may be actualizing their goals for diversity and inclusion but may find that the new chair leads differently than men who came before her [6]. This new type of leadership may cause disruption and even backlash if the college dean and provost are unprepared. Most of us do not like change but will go along with it unless it introduces new demands on our familiar practices and creates too much discomfort or other forms of dissonance. In systems that promote individualism, a woman leader who fosters teamwork and more collaborations may not be positively received.

In higher education, there is a heightened focus on the advancement of persons of color into leadership positions to demonstrate inclusivity, role models, and progressiveness. This is often a double-edged sword for the leader, competent for the role but now overseeing a staff that has never reported to a woman of color [5, 6]. Some individuals may try to delegitimize the leader, challenging her authority and even undermining her. Although organizational DEIA initiatives are key to promoting dignity and respect by positioning people for success, to do so without sufficient preparation for a change in the culture can prove harmful to individuals [4].

To engage in successful diversity management strategies requires a specific focus on personal and organizational culture, cultural differences, culture change, and relationship building [21]. Many organizations have hired consultants to guide and support their DEIA initiatives. Creating a climate of inclusion requires intentionality, education and training, and assessment of impact and sustainability. Cultural competency development is one framework being applied in organizations that say they want to address microaggressions or unconscious bias, as one example. This framework is based on the multicultural counseling competency (MCC) paradigm of *awareness, knowledge, and skills* [49]. Developed originally for application for interpersonal clinical counseling interactions, the paradigm also has relevance to organizations that want to put DEI principles into practice.

Multicultural organizational development applying the MCC is underway in universities. One example is a university's intention to hire and retain more underrepresented faculty, staff, and administrators. In consultation with an external consulting team, they developed a train-the-trainer (T3) program addressing their desired goals for hiring and retention based on the cultural competency framework. The T3 professionals included department chairs, senior faculty, and administrators from the provost's office typically involved in hiring processes. Deans and other senior administrators attended workshops to preview the program that would be delivered in their respective colleges. This all-inclusive process was designed to promote openness, interdependence across colleges, shared responsibility for the institutional hiring and retention goals, and sustainability.

Finally, for institutions who wish to embark on DEI initiatives, they should keep in mind that this is a long-term, change-related commitment. Many universities have learned that bringing in one individual of color or one woman to an academic department does not mean they are promoting equity, particularly if the individual leaves, is not promoted, or finds the department does not really encourage inclusion. Multicultural organizational development is aspirational and necessary in the twenty-first century to be culturally responsive to the demographic pipelines into higher education from Latinx, Asian, Black, American Indian, LGBTQ, and persons with disabilities. Leaders need to take heed of approaches and practices that can ensure greater success for their DEI goals.

One final consideration relates to applying the Dimensions of Personal Identity model [8] previously discussed and its relevance to multicultural organizational development. "Organizations and people are in interdependent relationships" ([4], p. 11). It behooves institutions to recognize how they foster the success of individuals and groups of different social identities. Statements about valuing DEI will fall short without intentional actions to make a change so that all individuals can benefit from the institutions they serve.

Structural and Systemic Dynamics and Practices Adversely Affecting Women

For many years, the "isms" have been part of organizational behavior with systems disadvantaging individuals as a result of ageism, racism, sexism, homophobia, linguicism, and disability status. In cultural competency development discussions, the isms are markers that lead to prejudice, stereotyping, and discrimination in organizations. This is also referred to as systemic sexism and racism because deficit attitudes have become codified into hiring and promotion practices, salary differentials between men and women, and other forms of discrimination. As universities attend more to DEI goals in their departments and colleges, they are also unmasking the prevalence of White privilege and prejudices toward women, African Americans, and other ethnic/racial minority faculty and staff. Specific to women, isms have diminished women and created systemic barriers to access participation and advancement.

From social psychology, different terms relate to attributions, labeling, and titling that often take on a negative gender-centric meaning in universities and other work settings. These meanings can become internalized and become embedded in organization systems and practices that others begin to apply to a woman. In this discussion, references will be made to the Dimensions of Personal Identity because this model of intersecting and historic-gendered attributions supports the examples provided herein.

To begin with, some historical stereotypes and values often lead to pigeon-hole practices, diminish, and cause women to leave academic positions. Although these practices are also evident in corporate settings, higher education issues are now beginning to provide evidence-based voices. For example, when women are assumed inexperienced or incapable of leading a research team, they are relegated to serve as assistants or on teams with graduate students. These practices speak to stereotypes and presumed incompetence of women as not possessing qualities to work independently and lead/supervise. In *Presumed Incompetent* [42], women in the academy from different intersecting identities relate the feedback, both verbal and nonverbal, that presumes them to be incompetent. For doctoral students and STEM professionals in the academy, these situations present double binds as well as perhaps self-doubts. The imposter syndrome may reappear, causing women to question their place in the academy. Another intrapersonal psychological phenomenon that may emerge is stereotype threat [48] whereby women who have internalized a belief that they are not meant for the world of STEM, despite their accomplishments and preparation, begin to self-doubt. Eagly and Chin [18] reported that women of color often receive less affirming feedback about their intellectual talent than their White counterparts. These double standards for women of color also introduce double binds. Women, in general, have been socialized to not self-promote. Still, when a woman of color has no advocates, she may have to decide to engage in self-advocacy and risk the possibility that others will see her as a braggart. Retribution for speaking up may lead to stigma, the disapproval of a person because she has stepped out of her expected gendered role. Another perception of a self-assured woman may be that of role congruence violations [53]. If women are expected to remain silent and follow a man's lead, speaking up may be viewed unfavorably.

Assimilation is generally expected in higher education culture. Although a woman may have been hired for her unique research focus, to fit in, women must follow the prescribed values and norms of a department to succeed. For women of color and international women who speak English as a second language, the culture of White male privilege is an automatic barrier, and tokenism may follow. Women report having to navigate the workplace with diplomacy, mistrust, and hypervigilance [5]. Power and privilege are often ascribed to White men readily. This unearned power does not apply to women in general. Commonly not acknowledged is that women of color have lower ascribed status than White women, regardless of their position, which means their behavior—communication interactions, expressions of self-confidence, and use of power—may be scrutinized and assessed differently. Although gender is not an innate, stable characteristic of a person, it still exists and is politically relevant and consequential. In higher education, *positionality* exists and asks people to understand and describe how gender and other identity markers inform how we see the world around us [44]. To not "honor" positionality, an unwritten rule means that women of color may run afoul of established norms and demonstrate role congruence violations.

Intersectional invisibility often occurs for women [15]. That is, for White women, only their gender is recognized versus their total being as tenured full professors with a degree from UCLA, in a same-sex relationship, and originally from Tulsa, OK. Alternatively, perhaps her lesbian identity becomes more noteworthy in a predominantly male heterosexual environment. An African American department chair in engineering with a degree from Harvard, a Fellow with NASEM, mother, and originally from Seattle, may be noticed first for her visible color. Without truly knowing the woman's identity, other scientists may make assumptions about her presence in a given setting or her assertiveness in different conversations. As Janet Helms has written [29], persons of visible ethnic/racial group identity are held up to higher standards and often deemed questionable in visible roles of authority.

Sexism, ageism, and racism in higher education continue to contribute to the "chilly climate" reported by many women (Sandler 1984), and systemic incidents of racism and sexism are commonplace. In *Presumed Incompetent* [42], there are multiple accounts of barriers to promotion and advancement, recognition, appointments to essential university committees, and other intentional ways to marginalize women of color. When women of color assume leadership roles, it is not unusual for colleagues to try to sabotage. Silencing women and women of color is a common practice [35]. An example is a Latina tenured full professor and a new director of an academic center for women's studies. Professor Lillian learned the first week that a male senior faculty member wanted her space. He believed that it was more than she needed for the team, although the previous director, a White male who had a social research center, had the space for 10 years. She planned carefully with her team in whom she confided. When an open forum occurred with the space issue on the agenda, her team took charge; the center space remained. Professor Lillian reported the tensions she experienced and the emotional intelligence she had to apply to keep her cool; it was a test of courage and self-efficacy [6].

Agency or a sense of agency is a concept that may describe the self-efficacy of the women, also demonstrating resonant leadership. A psychological term, sense of agency refers to an individual's cognitive thought process about what she believes she can do and can actually do [16]. Others have talked about agency as behavior demonstrating that one assumes responsibility and influences one's own life [39]. In doing so, individuals are also developing resilience to manage challenging and stressful situations, both personally and professionally. By so doing, they grow in self-respect. The Sense of Agency Scale [52] is based on the premise that a person is the initiator of her/his actions. Anticipation, control, and attention to the environment are central considerations for a sense of agency.

Sexual Misconduct and Harassment in Higher Education

In 1986, the Supreme Court ruled that a hostile work environment could be invoked in sexual harassment cases. Specific to higher education, Title IX is often applied because it prohibits sex discrimination in education programs receiving federal support. Equity with the distribution of sports programs for women and men is a criterion for the NCAA as well as federal agencies that provide funding to institutions of higher learning.

Thanks again to the #metoomovement, and complaints filed against Harvey Weinstein, the cover-ups on sexual harassment in the academy have gained more visibility. In 2018, for example, *The Chronicle of Higher Education* published a listing of 22 institutions mentioned once as having reported sexual harassment [12, 22]. A smaller group was posted as universities that had been cited more than once for complaints brought against them. Among the latter was the University of Wisconsin at Milwaukee that had 40 reported cases. Of these, 11 were confirmed violations; however, according to the report, only 1 case had been reported by the Wisconsin system in 20 years [22, 55]. Extensive coverage by Gluckman et al. [22] began in 2017 with an article in *The Chronicle of Higher Education* updated in 2018, citing more institutions and specifics about sexual harassment. Herein, they reported on complaints, findings, dismissals, and pending cases across the country. Incidents that date back to 2000 and earlier include the names of the accused and disposition of the matter if there is one. Not all sexual harassment occurs in the sciences, engineering, and medicine, but a higher percentage seems to come from these disciplines and senior well-regarded male professors. The authors point to structural and cultural conditions in the academy, particularly in disciplines where women are underrepresented, such as astronomy and philosophy, as more hostile.

Contradictions abound when incidents in the social sciences are reported. Bullying occurs in the humanities and other fields where research on critical race theory, women's studies, and other social identities are examined. In an article on abusers and enablers in the academy, Amienne [3] cited four reasons sexual harassment persists. First, she inferred from conversations with victims that abusers both charm and manipulate the victim, confusing them about the rewarding and abusive behavior. As with dysfunctional families and relationships, in the academy, there are enablers, individuals, often with power, who allow the perpetrator to continue to harm because of an existing working relationship from which they mutually benefit. Alternatively, the department chair enables the "do not rock the boat" posture. Third, from a systems perspective, she points to another reason—"it is easier to blame the victim than change the system." Others cite how important it is to attend to institutional research awards, budget planning, and enrollments rather than sexual harassment complaints. "Abuse is normalized" and is fundamental to the failure of institutions to address the issue systemically. Amienne concludes that being good liberals is not going to change abuse and enablers.

The Persistence of Sexual Misconduct

Tackling sexual harassment in higher education has been and persists in spite of legal consequences, payments made to victims, scandalous headlines smearing an institution's reputation, and the victimization of students and faculty alike, particularly women. Yahnke [55] summarizes issues and reports related to sexual misconduct and harassment and its persistence, with a #metoomovement timeline emanating from Hollywood and the hospitality industry. Yahnke's review cataloged articles posted about cases that emerged between 2017 and 2018, citing that cases emerged at 23 institutions in the 4 months after charges were brought against Harvey Weinstein. As with the latter, abuse of power of students and faculty was prevalent. From academics, the concerns were the institutions' responses or lack of responses. At the time, the priority was external funding, meeting enrollment demands, and hiring stellar faculty; addressing sexual misconduct and sexual harassment complaints were put to the side.

The financial and reputational costs of lawsuits are becoming public. A 2016 lawsuit against the University of Tennessee brought a $2.5 million settlement, the largest to date for sexual misconduct by male athletes [11]. In the suit, six women alleged that the university fostered an environment that perpetuated sexual misconduct and assaults. It was also reported that 22 public universities paid more than $10.5 million for mishandling of claims. This suggests the institutions were not well-prepared internally to respond to complaints or take them seriously [37]. Yahnke goes on to query, *Why is it such a widespread problem?* She answers her own question by noting power differentials in higher education institutions, the structures in place, and the pervasive male-centric culture.

Sexual Harassment in the Sciences

A consensus study from the National Academies of Sciences, Engineering, and Medicine investigated the impact of sexual harassment in academia. *Sexual Harassment of Women: Climate, Culture, and Consequences in Academic Sciences, Engineering, and Medicine* [43] was a comprehensive analysis about the existing situation and changes needed to the culture and climate in universities of higher education, specifically in the sciences. The authors pointed to historic cultural and climate factors in the academy that contribute to high incidents of sexual harassment. In the sciences, these include male-dominated departments, the concentration of power bases in units that relegate students and junior faculty to a dependency status for their career advancement, symbolic and ineffective policies to prevent sexual harassment, and ill-informed leadership in a unit and throughout the institution to address the seriousness of sexual harassment.

Based on their investigation and findings from other research studies, the authors highlighted that "more than 50 percent of women faculty and staff report having been harassed" ([43], p. 1). With respect to students, there were similarly high rates falling into the 20–50% range. The reasons for students' incidents came from behavior by faculty/staff. It was reported that "women students in academic medicine experience more frequent sexual harassment than those in science and engineering" ([43], p.2).

The report [43] cites a 2018 study of the University of Texas system, in which female students studying science, engineering, and medicine reported experiencing sexual harassment at high rates. In that survey, about 20% of female science students as well as "more than a quarter of female engineering students and more than 40% of female medical students experienced sexual harassment" from university faculty and staff, the report states. When women are harassed, they are not likely to report it. In fact, reporting the issue is the least common response, according to the report. They also called attention to a report out of the Pennsylvania State University system. They argued that "high rates of harassment in academia, especially in STEM fields, damage the integrity of research…harassment is to blame in these areas of study" [43]. It calls for a change in the culture of academia, not just university policies. "In environments that are perceived as tolerant or permissive of sexual harassment," the authors write, "women are more likely to be directly harassed."

The authors observed, as did Rossiter in her studies of early women scientists, that women may have dropped out rather than report on their situation. In the 2018 report, multiple losses as a result of unmanaged institutional sexual harassment were cited. The first is the loss of women's talent and, as a result, losses to the advancement of the country's "economic and social well-being" ([43], p.2). In an NSF study of engineers, researchers found that women persist and leave the profession for varying reasons. Still, gender discrimination they experienced as students and later as professionals in the academy promoted their departure.

The Double Bind for Women of Color

In 2011, the American Association for the Advancement of Science issued a statement on the advancement and challenges for women of color in the sciences [28, 40]. Their statement came from a series of studies generated from a symposium of the *Harvard Educational Review*, 35 years after the initial gathering in 1975. Dorothy Malcolm, an original attendee in 1975 and director of AAAS Education and Human Resources, was the lead author of a 1976 study, "The Double Bind: The Price of Being a Minority Woman in Science" [41]. In their new analysis, 30 scientists from diverse fields identified changes in enrollment and graduation of women of color since the early 1970s, the increase yet low representation in part-time and full-time faculty status, and the presence of women of color particularly in community colleges where instruction versus research was the priority. They also pointed to the small gains made over the 30 years and found that the environment for women of color in higher education continued to create obstacles and adversities. Among the barriers identified were low visibility and isolation in their home units; "challenges to their authority, teaching competency, and scholarly expertise in the classroom" [40]; and emotional challenges in the face of negativity and adversity. The authors of the report indicated that institutions are often at fault for not providing a supportive environment and recognizing the talent of women who have had to negotiate multiple obstacles to arrive at doctoral programs and teaching positions.

STEM Women in the Academy: Opportunities and the Labyrinth

The sciences are representative of many other fields and industries that have positioned women as the "other" and outsiders contributing to what is today a lack of visible women in leadership roles in this country. Although the focus of this book is primarily women in the sciences, it is necessary to describe the broader societal values that influence the treatment of women in the workplace and higher education in particular. These values that persist are grounded in White, male, heterosexist hegemonic principles of superiority and dominance of the other sex and of others who do not fit the dominant group—visible ethnic and racial group members, individuals of LGBTQ identity status, and White men who are not representative of the alpha male.

The opportunities for women to enter the academy and to remain in the academy are complex. It is often argued that STEM faculty prefer to hire more qualified women over equally qualified men. Though women and men may have the same credentials, men are those hired.

To confront the chilly climate in academia, universities have partnered with the National Science Foundation for the past 20 years to provide programs that support STEM women through mentorship and other deliberate interventions. The initial program was POWRE, created in 1997, a fellowship program for individual women, providing support during their pre-tenure years. Subsequently, ADVANCE was established in 2001, making awards at three levels: (a) fellowships, (b) leadership, and (c) institutional transformation [36]. The institutional awards address faculty mentoring, dual-career hiring programs, pay equity studies, and family-friendly practices.

The NSF Broadening Participation Initiative is another program to foster the inclusion of underrepresented groups and diverse institutions. The latter include Historically Black Colleges and Universities, Hispanic-serving Institutions, and Tribal Colleges. Through HBCU-Up, funding has been secured to prepare women, primarily at the associate professor level, for academic leadership advancement at their institutions. The Excellence in Research (EiR) program supports faculty to support STEM education and research through the HBCU-up program.

Diversity, Equity, and Inclusion in the Workplace

Dating back to the 1970s, there have been passive and intentional efforts to increase the number of women in higher education, the academy, and other work settings. The Equal Opportunity Commission (EOC) was established in 1967 to regulate the hiring of women and persons of color. Affirmative Action became the program to address the hiring processes and reporting back to the EOC. However, Affirmative

Action had a negative connotation, and individuals were often labeled Affirmative Action hires, with presumptions that they were only hired because of their identity status. The term "qualified" was commonly used in position announcements, suggesting that potential underrepresented hires were not qualified. Presumptions of under-preparation were pervasive, and individuals were often labeled "twofers," hiring because of their gender and ethnic/racial minority status. In higher education, lawsuits ensued in Texas (the Bakke case) and California with allegations that students of color were taking the place of White persons, particularly in medical school admissions. Lawsuits ensued about using ethnic and racial identity as criteria for admissions.

Universities have pursued initiatives for diversity, equity, and inclusion for many reasons. Among these are goals to ensure that underrepresented individuals are recruited and retained and eventually promoted and tenured. Goals to address pay inequities between men and women and how to reduce the chilly climate include the use of microaggressions, increased tenure and promotion of underrepresented faculty, and unmasking sexual harassment and discrimination. Retaining STEM women is a priority, and NSF's intentional initiatives are providing the resources and mentorship needed to be promoted and tenured. Data will be instructive in the next few years.

References

1. *2018–2019 The State of Women in Academic Medicine: Exploring Pathways to Equity.* (2020). The Association of American Medical Colleges. https://www.aamc.org/data-reports/data/1-2019-state-women-academic-medicine-exploring-pathways-equity
2. *A Brief History of Mens and Womens Work.* (n.d.). Energy Enlighten. Retrieved July 29, 2020, from https://www.energyenlighten.com/a-brief-history-of-mens-and-womens-work
3. Amienne, K. a. (2017, November 2). Abusers and enablers in faculty culture. *The Chronicle of Higher Education.* https://www.chronicle.com/article/AbusersEnablers-in/241648
4. Arredondo, P. (1996). *Successful diversity management initiatives: A blueprint for planning and implementation.* SAGE Publications.
5. Arredondo, P. (2011). The "borderlands" experience for women of color as higher education leaders. In J. L. Martin (ed.), *Women as Leaders in Education: Succeeding Despite Inequity, Discrimination, and Other Challenges [2 volumes]: Succeeding Despite Inequity, Discrimination, and Other Challenges* (pp. 275–298). ABC-CLIO.
6. Arredondo, P. (2019). Latinx women aspiring, persisting, and maintaining cultural integrity. In P. A. Perez (ed.), *The Tenure-Track Process for Chicana and Latina Faculty: Experiences of Resisting and Persisting in the Academy* (pp. 106–129). Taylor & Francis.
7. Arredondo, P. (2020). Geert Hofstede. In B. J. Carducci & C. Nave (Eds.), *The Wiley encyclopedia of personality and individual differences, 4 volume set.* Wiley.
8. Arredondo, P., & Glauner, T. (1992). *Personal dimensions of identity model.* Empowerment Workshops, Inc.
9. Bahn, K. (2013, December 6). *The rise of the lady adjuncts | Chronicle Community.* The Chronicle of Higher Education. https://community.chronicle.com/news/206-the-rise-of-the-lady-adjuncts

10. Britton, D. M. (2017). Beyond the chilly climate: The salience of gender in women's academic careers. *Gender & Society, 31*(1), 5–27. https://doi.org/10.1177/0891243216681494.
11. Busta, H. (2018, September 21). *What one professor's list of 700 sexual misconduct cases means for higher ed.* Education Dive. https://www.educationdive.com/news/what-one-professors-list-of-700-sexual-misconduct-cases-means-for-higher-e/532897/
12. *Campus Sexual Assault Under Investigation.* (n.d.). The Chronicle of Higher Education. Retrieved May 18, 2020, from http://projects.chronicle.com/titleix/
13. Ceci, S. J., & Williams, W. M. (2015). Women have substantial advantage in STEM faculty hiring, except when competing against more-accomplished men. *Frontiers in Psychology, 6.* https://doi.org/10.3389/fpsyg.2015.01532.
14. Cheeseman Day, J. (2018, May 8). *Number of women lawyers at record high but men still highest earners.* The United States Census Bureau. https://www.census.gov/library/stories/2018/05/women-lawyers.html
15. Crenshaw, K. (2017). *On intersectionality: essential writings.* New Press, New York.
16. Duggins, S. D. (2011). *The development of sense of agency* [Georgia State University]. https://scholarworks.gsu.edu/psych_theses/88
17. Eagly, A., & Carli, L. L. (2007, September 1). Women and the labyrinth of leadership. *Harvard Business Review, September 2007.* https://hbr.org/2007/09/women-and-the-labyrinth-of-leadership
18. Eagly, A. H., & Chin, J. L. (2010). Diversity and leadership in a changing world. *American Psychologist, 65*(3), 216–224. https://doi.org/10.1037/a0018957.
19. Finkelstein, M. J., Conley, V. M., & Schuster, J. H. (2016). *The faculty factor: Reassessing the American Academy in a turbulent era.* Johns Hopkins University Press Books.
20. Flaherty, C. (2016, August 22). *Study finds gains in faculty diversity, but not on the tenure track.* https://www.insidehighered.com/news/2016/08/22/study-finds-gains-faculty-diversity-not-tenure-track
21. Fouad, N. A., & Arredondo, P. (2007). *Becoming culturally oriented: Practical advice for psychologists and educators.* American Psychological Association.
22. Gluckman, N., Read, B., Mangan, K., & Quilantan, B. (2017, November 13). Sexual harassment and assault in higher ed: What's happened since Weinstein. *The Chronicle of Higher Education.* https://www.chronicle.com/article/Sexual-HarassmentAssault/241757
23. Goldstein, J. (2001). *Transcending boundaries: Boston's Catholics and Jews, 1929–1965* [Brandeis University]. https://www.bc.edu/content/dam/files/research_sites/cjl/texts/cjrelations/resources/articles/goldstein.htm
24. Hall, E. (1976). *Beyond Culture.* Doubleday: Anchor Press.
25. Hall, E. T., & Hall, M. R. (1990). *Understanding cultural differences: Germans, French and Americans.* Quercus.
26. Hall, R. M., & Sandler, B. R. (1982). *The classroom climate: A chilly one for women?* https://eric.ed.gov/?id=ED215628
27. Hall, R. M., & Sandler, B. R. (1984). *Out of the classroom: A chilly campus climate for women?* https://eric.ed.gov/?id=ED254125
28. Hammonds, E. M. (2011, June 29). *35 years after the double bind: The price of being a minority woman in science.* Harvard Education Publishing Group. https://www.hepg.org/blog/35-years-after-the-double-bind-the-price-of-being
29. Helms, J. (1990).
30. Hofstede, G., Hofstede, G. J., & Minkov, M. (2010). *Cultures and organizations: Software of the mind* (3rd ed.). McGraw Hill Professional.
31. Hofstede, G., & Hofstede, H., Geert H. (1991). *Cultures and organizations: Software of the mind* (1st ed.). McGraw-Hill.
32. Italiano, L. (2020, January 10). *Women are now the majority of US workforce: Feds.* New York Post. https://nypost.com/2020/01/10/there-are-now-more-woman-in-the-workforce-than-men-feds/

33. Jensen, L. E., & Deemer, E. D. (2019). Identity, campus climate, and burnout among under-graduate women in STEM fields. *The Career Development Quarterly, 67*(2), 96–109. https://doi.org/10.1002/cdq.12174.
34. Kagan, J. (2019, October 24). *Glass Ceiling.* Investopedia. https://www.investopedia.com/terms/g/glass-ceiling.asp
35. Kanter, R. M. (1977). *Men and women of the corporation: New edition.* Basic Books.
36. Kempf, M. (2002, September 20). EmPOWREment and ADVANCEment for women: NSF pro-grams for women in science. *Science Magazine.* https://www.sciencemag.org/careers/2002/09/empowrement-and-advancement-women-nsf-programs-women-science
37. Korn, M. (2018, June 6). Schools pay millions in sexual-harassment set-tlements. *The Wall Street Journal.* https://www.wsj.com/articles/schools-pay-millions-in-sexual-harassment-settlements-1528277400
38. Kroeber, A. L., & Kluckhohn. (1952). *Culture: A Critical Review of Concepts and Definitions.* Fb&c Limited.
39. Lamia, M. C. (2010, October 15). Your sense of agency: Influencing your own life and taking responsibility. *Psychology Today.* http://www.psychologytoday.com/blog/the-white-knight-syndrome/201010/your-sense-agency-influencing-your-own-life-and-taking
40. Lempinen, E. W. (2011, August 14). Thirty-five years after "The Double Bind," Obstacles remain for minority women in STEM. *American Association for the Advancement of Science.* https://www.aaas.org/news/thirty-five-years-after-double-bind-obstacles-remain-minority-women-stem-0
41. Malcom, S. M., Paula Q. Hall, & Janet W. Brown. (1976). *The double bind: The price of being a minority woman in science. Report of a conference of Minority Women Scientists, Arlie House, Warrenton, Virginia.* American Association for the Advancement of Science, 1515 Massachusetts Avenue, N. https://eric.ed.gov/?id=ED130851
42. Muhs, G. G., Niemann, Y. F., & González, C. G. (2012). *Presumed incompetent: The inter-sections of race and class for women in academia* (A. P. Harris, Ed.). University Press of Colorado.
43. National Academies of Sciences, Engineering, and Medicine, Policy and Global Affairs, Committee on Women in Science, Engineering, and Medicine, & Committee on the Impacts of Sexual Harassment in Academia. (2018). *Sexual harassment of women: climate, culture, and consequences in academic sciences, engineering, and medicine* (F. F. Benya, S. E. Widnall, & P. A. Johnson, Eds.). National Academies Press (US). http://www.ncbi.nlm.nih.gov/books/NBK507206/
44. *Positionality—Dictionary.Com.* (n.d.). Retrieved August 2, 2020, from Https://www.Dictionary.Com/E/Gender-Sexuality/Positionality/
45. Sandler, B. R. (1999). The chilly climate: Subtle ways in which women are often treated dif-ferently at work and in classrooms. *National Alliance for Partnerships in Equity (NAPE), 8*(3), 7.
46. Shen, X., & Tian, X. (2012). Academic culture and campus culture of universities. *Higher Education Studies, 2*(2), 61–65.
47. Simplicio, J. (2012). The University Culture. *Education, 133*(2), 336–339.
48. Steele, C. M. (1998, July 1). *Stereotyping and its threat are real.* American Psychologist; US: American Psychological Association. https://doi.org/10.1037/0003-066X.53.6.680
49. Sue, D. W., Arredondo, P., & McDavis, R. J. (1992). Multicultural counseling competencies and standards: A call to the profession. *Journal of Multicultural Counseling and Development, 20*(2), 64–88. https://doi.org/10.1002/j.2161-1912.1992.tb00563.x.
50. Sumra, M. K., & Schillaci, M. A. (2015). Stress and the multiple-role woman: Taking a closer look at the "Superwoman". *PLOS ONE, 10*(3). https://doi.org/10.1371/journal.pone.0120952.
51. Tannen, D. (1990). *You just don't understand: Women and men in conversation.* Harper Collins.
52. Tapal, A., Oren, E., Dar, R., & Eitam, B. (2017). The sense of agency scale: A measure of con-sciously perceived control over one's mind, body, and the immediate environment. *Frontiers in Psychology, 8.* https://doi.org/10.3389/fpsyg.2017.01552

53. Toosi, N. R., Mor, S., Semnani-Azad, Z., Phillips, K. W., & Amanatullah, E. T. (2019). Who can lean in? The intersecting role of race and gender in negotiations. *Psychology of Women Quarterly, 43*(1), 7–21. https://doi.org/10.1177/0361684318800492.

54. Welter, B. (1966). The Cult of True Womanhood, 1820–1860. *American Quarterly*, 157–174.

55. Yahnke, K. (2019, January 30). *The 2020 guide to workplace sexual harassment*. I-Sight. https://i-sight.com/resources/guide-to-workplace-sexual-harassment-infographic/

Chapter 4
Qualitative Methodology: Thematic Analysis

This study's objective was to query women's experiences in academic STEM environments – namely, to explore what factors lead to persisting (or not) along the academic pathways in the sciences. The interview questions invited the women from diverse backgrounds to reflect on their experiences and provide examples of situations, relationships, and hopes for their careers and that of other women in STEM. The proposed demographic was women who currently hold an academic position in a STEM field – administrators, staff, and faculty (tenured, tenure track, and nontenure track). The study was conducted remotely (i.e., online and via telephone) so that women from all over the USA could be recruited and participate. The IRB approved the study at Teachers College, Columbia University, the home institution for two authors.

Feminist Methodology

The qualitative methodology applied for this study is informed by principles from feminist psychology, emphasizing the value of learning and developing knowledge directly from women's voices. Standpoint theory [1, 3] speaks to an epistemology that leads to an inclusive scholarship from the margins versus the researchers' top-down perspectives. Standpoint theorists invite sharing from subjective experiences, questioning the use of methodology described as neutral and objective. Harding asserted that methodology inclusive of marginalized persons and groups would likely create new knowledge that is more relevant and applicable for specific and broad contexts and issues.

© The Author(s), under exclusive license to Springer Nature Switzerland AG 2022
P. Arredondo et al., *Women and the Challenge of STEM Professions*, International
and Cultural Psychology, https://doi.org/10.1007/978-3-030-62201-5_4

Procedure

Study invitations were sent via email through related list-servs (e.g., 500 women scientists), directly to STEM departments, and directly to known contacts who then shared the list with others (i.e., snowball method). Women who consented to participate were then invited to complete a demographic questionnaire (found in Table 4.1), followed by a brief open-ended questionnaire querying their career experiences in the sciences (found in Table 4.2). The study was originally designed to be mixed-method. Those who completed the questionnaire were given an option to be interviewed for 30–40 min by one of the researchers in an effort to gain a deeper and more dimensional understanding of their responses. However, the ten participants who completed the questionnaire also elected to be interviewed, and as such only interview data was analyzed and is reported herein. The semi-structured protocol used to interview participants can be found in Table 4.3. All interviews were conducted over the phone by one of the authors, recorded (with consent), and later transcribed verbatim.

Upon completing the demographic and open-ended questionnaire, each participant (N = 10) offered to be contacted for a follow-up interview. The authors each interviewed two or three participants following the same semi-structured protocol. Verbatim transcripts were shared among the authors as soon as they were available.

Table 4.1 Demographic questions

Gender identity:	Age:	Ethnicity:
Relationship status:	Children:	
Place of birth:	Parent's occupation:	
Terminal degree:	Area of study:	
Institution:		
Current position:	Number of years in this field:	
Tenure status (if applicable):	Institution:	
Previous position:	Number of years:	
Tenure status (if applicable):	Institution:	
Have you ever had an administrative role? If so, what was the title and what was the scope of responsibility?		
Recognitions/awards (i.e., fellow, member of a STEM academy):		
Grant awards ($):		

Table 4.2 Questionnaire protocol

1. Why did you decide to pursue a STEM degree? Motivators, mentors, ideals?
2. When you think about your career to date, what are some aspects of both your journey and current position that you feel good about?
3. When you think about your career to date, what are some aspects of both your journey and current position that have been negative and/or disappointing?
4. As a woman in STEM, what have been the advantages? What have been the disadvantages?
5. Some women describe their work environment as a "chilly climate." How does this resonate with you?

Table 4.3 Semi-structured interview protocol

1. Why are you choosing to participate in the interview itself? What are your reasons?
2. How did you arrive at higher education as a career track?
3. Describe your experiences in advancing with your career plans.
4. Describe your experiences in not advancing with your career plans.
5. Who have been your advocates?
6. Describe the attributes of a "healthy" workplace; "unhealthy" workplace. What are your personal experiences?
7. Has anyone, or anything, blocked your path?
8. In your estimation, what institutional structures support or prevent the advancement of women in STEM?
9. In higher education and other work environments, the term "microaggressions" often comes up. Please share your experiences specific to microaggressions. What have been the effects?
10. What have been your strategies to manage the microaggressions?
11. Please share a few recommendations for women in graduate school and higher education deans and chairs.
12. If you could share recommendations with STEM deans and chairs, what would they be?

Participants

A total of ten (N = 10) women participated in this study. The mean age of the sample was 44 years old (SD = 9.44). Five (N = 5) self-identified as White, three (N = 3) as Hispanic/Latino, one (N = 1) as biracial – White and Hispanic/Latino – and one (N = 1) as Black American. Six (N = 6) were married, and four (N = 4) were single. Six (N = 6) had children. Two (N = 2) of the women were born outside of the USA. Three (N = 3) were tenured, three (N = 3) were on a tenure track, two (N = 2) were postdoctoral fellows, one (N = 1) was a full-time lecturer, and one (N = 1) was in an administrative position. All (N = 10) were currently at predominantly white Research 1 (R1) institutions, and all (N = 10) had earned a Ph.D. In terms of their current departments, four (N = 4) were Clinical Psychology, two (N = 2) were Biology, one (N = 1) was Industrial Engineering, one (N = 1) was Biochemistry, one (N = 1) was Rehabilitative Sciences, and one (N = 1) was Computer Science. A summary can be found in Table 4.4.

Analysis

Thematic analysis was the qualitative method used with the interview dataset. This is an ideal method for identifying and reporting patterns within the data [2]. A theoretical approach was utilized, meaning that the team was coding for a specific research question, namely, "what factors contribute to success or lack thereof for women in the academic STEM environments?" A key aspect of thematic analysis involves immersing oneself in the dataset. All authors were provided with interview transcripts and asked to familiarize themselves with the content and make notes on

Table 4.4 Participant demographics

Pseudonym	Age	Race/ethnicity	Marital status	Children	Current position
Emma	37	Hispanic/Latino	Married	0	Postdoctoral fellow
Olivia	55	Black	Married	4	Tenured, department chair
Ava	27	White	Single	0	Administrative officer
Isabella	44	Hispanic/Latino	Married	2	Assistant professor, tenure track
Sophia	54	White	Married	3	Full-time lecturer
Charlotte	n/a	Hispanic/Latino	Single	0	Postdoctoral fellow
Mia	46	White	Married	2	Tenured
Amelia	39	White	Married	2	Assistant professor, tenure track
Harper	50	White + Hispanic/Latino	Single	1	Tenured
Evelyn	39	White	Single	0	Assistant professor

Table 4.5 Coding process

Data Extract	Codes
Emma: And so I identified the professors that would, you know, that understood that: Hey, I'm first generation. I don't know what I'm doing. And they were maybe more patient with me. They were more willing to tell me things that maybe I didn't even explicitly ask for because I didn't know explicitly that I should be asking for that.	Dark Green: Support from Professors; Active Guidance Turquoise: Lack of direction for how to succeed in graduate school / a system with invisible requirements

their initial ideas. In this first step, each author was asked to read over transcripts multiple times and search for meaning and patterns without actually coding; this is referred to as active reading [2]. In the next step, data were organized into meaningful groups – our process involved manually color-coding segments that represented similar concepts. Each color signified a code, and when multiple patterns were present in one data extract, comments were made in the margins to identify the various codes. Table 4.5 provides an example.

Once the entire dataset was coded, a new document was created with coded extracts reorganized by color. Using the example from Table 4.5, all of the coded material representing forms of support and guidance was taken from each transcript and organized together into one document. With the content visually together in one place, it was easier to examine codes for overlap and see how they may combine to form themes [2]. In order to consider the relationship between codes and themes, a thematic map was creative to help further analyze and determine main level themes and subthemes. Although this map started rather complex, the process of reviewing themes by all authors resulted in a refinement of themes, and multiple themes were collapsed into each other. For example, we initially coded all data related to parenting and the work/life balance and created a theme called "the parenthood challenge." Through a review of themes in the entire dataset, however, it became clear that the data speaking to the balance challenge as it relates to parenthood was better captured by the larger theme of support – thus our original candidate theme of parenthood challenge became instead a subtheme of the main theme, support. We continued this process until (a) we reached consensus on themes, (b) we felt the thematic map accurately represented our entire dataset, and (c) we revisited the entire dataset as a whole and ensured there were no additional themes present. Figure 4.1 depicts the final thematic map for this study.

Fig. 4.1 Final thematic map

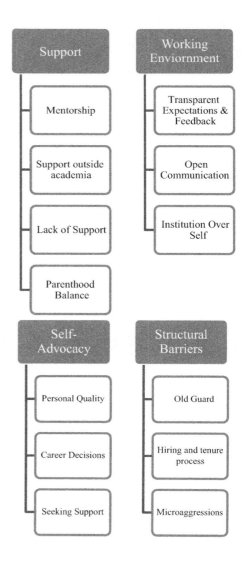

References

1. Borland, E. (2020, May 13). *Standpoint theory*. Encyclopedia Britannica. https://www.britannica.com/topic/standpoint-theory
2. Braun, V., & Clarke, V. (2006). Using thematic analysis in psychology. *Qualitative Research in Psychology, 3*(2), 77–101. https://doi.org/10.1191/1478088706qp063oa.
3. Smith, D. E. (1987). *The everyday world as problematic: A feminist sociology*. NorthEastern University Press.

Chapter 5
"Because You Can't Do It on Your Own": The Role of Support

A query of this study was to understand not only how participants arrived on their career path in higher education in STEM but also how they navigated the academic environment once they arrived. A central theme was that of support; all participants spoke to various forms of support (or lack thereof) as being crucial in their academic journeys and career trajectories.

Mentorship

All ten participants in this study independently identified mentors as being central to their success—and interestingly, all ten participants gave this answer in response to the initial question of, "How did you arrive at a career in higher education?" The protocol did not specifically query mentorship. Though the participants spoke to different experiences with mentors, there was universal agreement for the idea that mentors were crucial and an extremely important and influential source of support in their academic journeys.

Kram's [2] seminal work identified two major functions of mentorship: career functions and psychosocial functions. Whereas career functions relate to helping a mentee navigate advancement in the institution, psychosocial relates more to personal and professional growth—such as nurturing an academic identity and academic self-worth. Emma, a current postdoc, shared how instrumental her mentors were in illuminating the way forward from a career function perspective:

> And so I identified the professors that would, you know, that understood that: Hey, I'm first generation. I don't know what I'm doing. And they were maybe more patient with me. They were more willing to tell me things that maybe I didn't even explicitly ask for because I didn't know explicitly that I should be asking for that.

This participant is speaking to career functions—specifically to being told and shown how to successfully move through graduate school. She further described how mentorship as an undergraduate propelled her to graduate school:

> I had a specific professor who really encouraged me to do research, undergraduate research. And, you know, she gave me the application and she said, you know, these are things that you can do if you're interested. And just little things like that of showing interest and, and being proactive with, you know, providing information even if I didn't necessarily ask for it, I think was a really important.

All ten participants shared similar anecdotes of their undergraduate and graduate school professors "opening doors," "making connections," and "sharing or providing resources I did not know were there." Participants credit these mentoring relationships with their decisions to apply to graduate programs, postdoc programs, and academic faculty positions. There were more positive anecdotes (6) related to the undergraduate experience than graduate (4). Perhaps not surprising, effective mentoring at the graduate and postdoctoral stages in STEM fields has long been linked to performance, success, and career advancement [1].

Less frequently, participants spoke to the importance of mentorships in navigating the tenure process (three participants). A junior faculty member shared how her department chair sat her down when she first arrived to the institution and expressed the importance of grant writing in the tenure process:

> My chair was very clear about the fact that [grant writing is] probably the most important thing for me to be doing, how to spend my time right from day one. And so it was very clear advice. And so that was something that I just kept sticking to.

Sophia, currently a lecturer, discussed how she had been in a part-time role for so many years without benefits or tuition remission, and her department chair advocated for her when a new full-time position came up:

> And she knew a lot about my work and couldn't believe that I had been in a part time position all those years. And a full time senior lectureship had opened up in the university and she fought for me to get it, and I did. And for the first time, was finally eligible for benefits and for pension and health care and so on.

We clearly see the career function of the mentorship process at work in their descriptions. While learning to navigate academic environments is clearly important, participants also spoke to the importance of a mentoring relationship that was transparent and genuine and showed interest in their personal goals and growth. Recent research looking at the woman-woman mentoring relationship for tenure-track faculty finds that the holistic relationships (involving both advice/guidance and honesty and listening well) helped women faculty navigate the tenure process more effectively [4]. Participants spoke to these psychosocial functions of mentorship: "And, [the professor] she just always reminded me of, you know, that I was intelligent. That I was capable. And if there were difficulties, it wasn't necessarily because I couldn't do it." In this case, the mentor is nurturing the participant's academic identity and self-esteem and helping build her confidence for her ability to succeed in a graduate program. Similarly, a postdoc currently working in a research lab shared how much it impacted her when mentors took a personal interest in her work:

> But I've had like a couple of mentors and programs along the way—that have really boosted my development. And their interest in my academic learning—has also, in addition to my desire—to do science has both allowed me to be at this stage and beyond.

Mentors Outside of STEM Six of the ten participants specifically spoke to the importance of seeking mentorship and guidance outside of one's department, institution, and/or field of study. This external perspective was highly valued and attributed with making it possible for participants to succeed in various stages of their STEM academic journeys. For two participants, external mentorships served as sounding boards and objective perspectives:

> And then I've also sought out other women in completely different departments from across campus to kind of-, so they don't have that internal bias to what might be going on politically within my own department. And so I try to seek out women, experienced women, from different backgrounds and different locations within not only my institution but outside.

In addition to offering a lens apart from departmental politics, a tenured professor, Harper, identified the value in diverse perspectives, stating:

> Mentors are both within and outside of the institution...I guess earlier on in my career, but particularly in graduate school, I wasn't aware that one could do that. I thought you have to get everything just from one place and then it was only over time that I realized, oh, you can have all different types of mentors to broaden your horizons.

While some were seeking various forms of guidance and perspective for how to succeed on their chosen path, other participants found solace and the support needed to remain on their chosen path. For example, one participant discusses how three different professors, outside of STEM, were open with her about their own challenges during their doctoral work, and provided help whenever she needed it, without causing her to feel like she was unintelligent. To these professors, she attributes her success: "I would say those three professors during my doctoral program were just incredible. I mean, they were the reasons I didn't quit." Isabella recalls how important it was to look outside of the research lab during graduate school: "As a student, my naiveté was challenged and it was then that I reached for mentors to help me along the way, outside of the laboratory." Evelyn, a junior faculty member, has used the digital space to find a support group outside of her STEM department: She has a writing group where they read each other's work and provide feedback. This has been an important connection for her because she has not been able to find a similar-type group within her own department or even at her institution: "And so I've found it difficult for me personally at my own institution to find the support networks. So because of this, I've established my own virtually." Emma shared how she turned to coursework in education to validate her experiences as a woman of color in a graduate school STEM program where coursework was void of conversations related to race, racial identity, and other social identity groups: "I think that was also therapeutic and validating for me, to be able to read that literature. And I wouldn't—, I wouldn't have been exposed to that if I didn't proactively take courses in education." Here we see participants employing strategies for engendering support and building networks when none are immediately available in their places of work and study.

Lack of Support Within Mentoring While every participant had a positive mentoring relationship to share, there were also several narratives (5) depicting a lack of support and difficult or disappointing experiences with would-be mentors. Emma had a far more positive experience in undergraduate than in graduate study, sharing, "I felt not supported as a doctoral student, even when I would explicitly ask for it. And I would explicitly seek out different people. I just didn't feel that I got what I needed." Similarly, a participant shared that:

> [In undergrad] there were programs that promoted diversity in scientific fields. I was part of those programs…they allowed mentorship and also like financial support…So those programs were critical in college. And then in graduate school, there were no such programs.

This participant went on to share how contrasting her undergraduate experience was from her graduate program—a lack of programmatic support both fiduciary and relational made the graduate school process far more arduous and challenging for her. Indeed, studies support the idea that a lack of mentoring or ineffective mentoring relationship decreases productivity and increases stress among graduate students [1].

Olivia, newly promoted to department chair, shared similar sentiments of feeling a lack of support in this new position:

> Well, I mean, I was new to the position [as Department Chair] so—. It was good. I've had some bumps along the way because I had no guidance at all. Which was the downside to the position. No mentoring. You know? It was kind of like, here's your office. [laughter] Here's a chair.

Her narrative speaks to the importance of continued mentorship throughout one's academic career and each time one makes a new advancement in the field. This participant spoke to often feeling isolated and unsuccessful in her role due to a lack of internal support and guidance. Her story is not unlike those in this study that described feeling alone during graduate programs or on tenure tracks; their feelings of having no support were often compounded by also having a lack of direction for how to successfully proceed. This speaks to the idea that both professional and personal support are key to successfully navigating academic STEM environments.

Support Outside of Academia

Second to mentorship, participants spoke to the importance of having a strong external support system to get them through their academic journey in STEM. Four out of ten specifically named their partner as being a crucial influence on their success. For example, Sophia shared: "And, you know, I also had an incredibly supportive husband who very much did not want me to compromise my career or sanity. And who was himself, a very, very involved father and you know, equally involved person in managing the household and taking care of the kids." Amelia shared:

> My spouse, pretty much gave up his career for me to be able to do this. And I'm not sure. Well, actually I am pretty sure that if, if, if that weren't the case. I don't think that I would be able to be in this tenure track position.

In addition to naming spouses as making it possible to succeed in their career journeys, two participants spoke to the importance of partner support around recognizing unhealthy patterns and environments. Emma recalled, "And it took my partner to tell me just quit [the toxic lab]. And he supported me at the end." When Olivia felt isolated and faced interdepartmental adversity, she explained how her husband helped her persist and withstand a "toxic work environment" by being her "sanity check" and offering an objective perspective.

Two participants identified peer support as being critical in their graduate school STEM experiences. One was a postdoc, and the other had taken an administrative role in a STEM department. The postdoc shared, "I found a group of students that were willing to openly talk about how frustrated we were. How lost we felt…How difficult this all was. So that was one really important, I think, for me, it was that peer support." The other participant described how work in their research lab was not equally shared among participants and it was not until they got together outside the lab to talk that she realized how imbalanced the situation was. The peer network illuminated the unfair workload and helped her to take action in changing it:

> There was a group of us that were pretty close…And we ate lunch together, and, you know, sort of socialized outside of lab. And it came up that we were doing a lot of the, you know, work to keep the lab running. While maybe a couple of other notable people were not doing any work to keep the lab running but benefitting from all the work that we'd done. And so that was sort of a first realization that maybe something needed to change.

The ability to openly share frustrations and to talk through issues was crucial for both of these participants to move successfully through their respective STEM environments.

Social support has been positively associated with many academic and personal outcomes for graduate students and tenure-track faculty. Our participants placed a high value on mentor relationships both within and outside their STEM departments and credited these relationships with helping them to successfully navigate and persist in their academic journeys.

Parenthood Challenge: Support for the Work/Life Balance

Three of the participants in this study spoke to challenges related to becoming a parent and balancing either graduate school or tenure requirements. In all instances, participants discussed that one partner had to take a step back in order for the other to continue on their career track. In two cases, it was the participants' partners that stepped back to care for children. As Amelia shared, "And from the start it was kind of clear that we couldn't both have demanding careers. So his career took a backseat to mine...My spouse, pretty much gave up his career for me to be able to do this." Mia shared a similar story:

> After baby one, [my partner and I] were like, oh, this is hard. And after baby two—This is impossible. [laughter] Someone has to step back. And I just got lucky that, you know, I had a partner who was willing to step back.

In one case, it was the participant herself who took a step back. Sophia explains that she consciously exited the tenure track to make space for her marriage and children: "I made a very conscious decision to step off that superstar pathway because I wanted to have a marriage and kids that worked and that I love." In all three cases, participants were married to or dating partners who were also in academia. This is a well-documented issue—a book that explores survey data from tens of thousands of graduate students over their careers finds that it is extremely common for one partner to have to defer to the other for the sake of the other's career and that it is far more likely to be the woman who defers [3]. Mason et al. [3] describe a "baby penalty" that women in academia frequently have to pay, as child-rearing and tenure requirements often occur at the exact same time. One participant speaks directly to this phenomenon: "Just the fact that the push for tenure comes at exactly the height of a time in one's life when one is having small children. I mean, it's just the most awful confluence of sort of developmental crises for people."

Research shows that having babies and small children affects men and women's academic career paths differently—men with young children are 35% more likely than women with young children to secure tenure-track positions [5]. Further, female graduate students and postdoctoral fellows who have babies while students or fellows are more than twice as likely as new fathers or women who do not have children to turn away from an academic research career [3]. Participants in this study shared a feeling that paternity leaves tended to strengthen male candidates positions, whereas maternity leave often resulted in a woman never returning to the tenure track:

> Sophia: And the ways in which when men get parental leave, they typically use it to get more writing and research done. They treat it as a sabbatical. Whereas women don't. They treat it as an actual parental leave.
> Mia: The few small attempts that are made to accommodate women in academia seem to be benefitting men more. Like, oh, we're going to give family leave to everyone. And women take a family leave and take care of babies. And men take a family leave and they write papers.

All three participants also discussed a lack of resources for women in the field having children—they each specifically named a lack of pathways to reenter their professions as being a major barrier to remaining on a tenure track: "We need better support for child care...we need to give women the opportunity to re-enter if they leave for five years, because they actually do want to be with their babies, you know." The lack of support for female academics having babies during tenure years is well documented, and according to Mason et al. [3] who have contributed to both the popular press and scientific literature on the subject, the impact of the baby penalty on female faculty members in the sciences in particular is more decisive.

Both participants that remained on the tenure track while their partner stayed home to care for their children shared anecdotes of colleagues presuming them to be less capable. One shared: "When I had my first [baby] I wanted to TA this one class...And I talked to the professor. And he said something like: 'Well, sure. But I don't want to hear any kid excuses, because I have three'." Another recalled how "one colleague who told me very explicitly when I had my first baby that I shouldn't be doing this... because it would get in the way of my scholarly scholarly productivity." Messages come through colleagues, mentors, and the very structure of the system to suggest that caring for young children and succeeding through the tenure track are mutually exclusive [5]. Perhaps this is why adjunct and nontenure-track roles represent the fastest growing area in academia among women [6]. Our results support existing literature that suggests that academia (for both graduate students and tenure-track faculty) needs better support systems in place for women through childbirth and parenting.

References

1. Hund, A. K., Churchill, A. C., Faist, A. M., Havrilla, C. A., Stowell, S. M. L., McCreery, H. F., Ng, J., Pinzone, C. A., & Scordato, E. S. C. (2018). Transforming mentorship in STEM by training scientists to be better leaders. *Ecology and Evolution, 8*(20), 9962–9974. https://doi.org/10.1002/ece3.4527.
2. Kram, K. E. (1986). Mentoring at work: Developmental relationships in organizational life. *Human Resource Management, 25*(4), 639–644. https://doi.org/10.1002/hrm.3930250410.
3. Mason, M. A., Wolfinger, N. H., & Goulden, M. (2013). *Do babies matter?: Gender and family in the ivory tower*. New Brunswick: Rutgers University Press.
4. Palmer, E. M., & Jones, S. J. (2019). Woman-woman mentoring relationships and their roles in tenure attainment. *Journal of Women and Gender in Higher Education, 12*(1), 1–17. https://doi.org/10.1080/19407882.2019.1568264.
5. Waxman, S., & Ispa-Landa, S. (2016, February 11). Academia's "Baby Penalty." *US News*. https://www.usnews.com/opinion/knowledge-bank/articles/2016-02-11/academia-must-correct-systemic-discrimination-and-bias-against-mothers
6. Wolfinger, N. H. (2013, July 29). For female scientists, there's no good time to have children – The Atlantic. *The Atlantic*. https://www.theatlantic.com/sexes/archive/2013/07/for-female-scientists-theres-no-good-time-to-have-children/278165/

Chapter 6
"Providing That Safe Place": Attributes of an Unhealthy vs. Healthy Work Environment

Unhealthy Work Environments

When women enter male-dominated STEM fields, they may experience a "chilly climate" in which they feel unwelcome [2, 5]. When describing unhealthy environments, participants in this study relayed the following themes: (1) lack of transparency and feedback, (2) serving the institution at your own cost, (3) default to assistant role, and (4) workload not being shared.

Lack of Transparency and Feedback When asked about the attributes of an unhealthy work environment, more than half the participants (6) specifically named a lack of clear expectations and directions as prohibitive. Emma, a postdoc, discussed her experience in a research lab where sharing of information and communication was very limited. She described an environment that lacked clear expectations: "No assessment, no feedback, no discussion about if you're on the right track or if you should change this, because you're going to waste three months trying to do something that isn't necessary." She goes on to further describe how the lack of feedback on her research ideas and lack of direction created a feeling of discouragement from continuing on in research in her field (she ultimately pursued teaching):

> I felt discouraged from pursuing a traditional STEM research career…there just wasn't that communication. I would say that my experiences in that route were difficult. I would have scientific ideas, talk them with my PI, get little feedback on whether or not they were good. But then I'd hear that they were using those ideas that I had talked about and were being done by someone. I was like, wait a minute. I talked about that with him.

Charlotte, a current postdoctoral fellow, spoke to the lack of clear communication related to what is "right" and "wrong" in order to learn and make constructive changes: "A lot of passive aggressiveness I've seen is, and microaggressions, is that there's no clear communications between people. And things are said either through email or in the back end that do not promote a good environment." Another participant, Amelia, shared how when she first started in her tenure-track position no one shared the ins and outs of the department with her: "All the time I spent trying to figure things out when it would have been really nice to have someone say like just a really basic idea of, this is the situation and here's the basic information that you need to function as part of this department."

Serving the Institution at Your Own Cost Four of the ten participants spoke to serving the institution at their own cost which led to feelings of being taken advantage of. Ava, a current administrative officer, reported:

> We get emails in the middle of the night ... and even at my new job, there's been a little bit of a challenge there's sort of this, you know, expectation that you're always going to be available and that this is the only thing that you care about. But sometimes it means that you're, you know, sacrificing things that would be good for you in order for the boss to do better.

Similarly, Sophia, a full time lecturer, shared how she was expected to take on extra work without extra pay: "There were other senior faculty in the department who were exploitative and expected me to take on burdens that were not part of my job description and to mentor undergraduate honor students and so on, with no extra compensation." When that senior faculty retorted to her that faculty get paid to mentor undergraduate honor students, Sophia replied:

> That is absolutely not true. Of course [they] get paid for that. [They] get paid with promotion and recognition and tenure and I'm not eligible for any of those things. So it is exploitative for [them] to expect me to take that on when I'm getting paid a quarter of what a tenure track faculty in my position would be being paid.

Default to Assistant Role A default to an assistant role also seemed to develop for some participants (2). Amelia, a tenure-track participant, expressed: "I mean, there's no question when it comes to like volunteering to do stuff. Nobody wants to do or service and it's all the women who are doing stuff and none of the men who are doing stuff." Another participant mentioned her experience feeling this way as far back as graduate school:

> I feel like in grad school a lot of the time... We were, particularly women, sort of shifted into the, you know, planner category. Or like, the assistant category. A lot of us did, you know, the-, every time the lab planned an outing, for the planning, you know, we organized it.

This same participant goes on to mention other "housekeeping" responsibilities that were impressed upon women more than men: "You know, we kept the calendar. We made sure that lunch was ordered. And, you know, we planned parties. People were all bringing stuff. And even things like shopping for the lab." Communal behavior was expected of the women. This is in line with social role theory, which argues that expectations about men and women necessarily reflect status and power differences [1, 4].

Unshared Workload Four (4) participants described workloads that were dispro-portionate—taking on more tasks and responsibilities than others and expectations of doing more without more credit. Sophia reported these extra responsibilities can make folks feel "demoralized" because it can lead to feeling like a "second-class citizen." Participants discussed situations (research labs, graduate school assign-ments, volunteer positions for faculty) whereby they and other women often took on multiple tasks and roles without recognition or even a discussion of responsibilities and expectations. This leads to suggestions for ways to improve upon these inequi-table work conditions. Ava reported ideas that could be implemented to improve this: "Since I've left, they sort of developed a system where, you know, everyone has to do these tasks. That we keep track and make sure that everyone has a task before anyone has to do a second task." Another, Amelia, shared that "a very easy thing could be to just look at the composition of what different committees are and whose volunteering for things and having a little bit more equity with regard to why the same people are always doing all of the service."

Healthy Environments

In contrast to unhealthy environments that participants experienced, six participants described that healthy environments are those that explicitly state expectations, have transparent norms, and provide resources.

Transparent Norms and Expectations Participants expressed that, as opposed to unhealthy environments lacking transparency and clarity, healthy environments promoted transparent norms and expectations of all staff. Overall, participants spoke to the importance of having a clearly marked roadmap in place for how to succeed in that particular institution and department. Mia, a tenured professor, stated, "It's definitely nice to see people ahead of you who have similar attributes and appear to be successful. It's nice to have examples." Emma, a postdoc, stated that knowing about supportive resources available to faculty and staff was extremely important: "And having those be again explicitly stated. This is where you go if you have a problem. This is where you go if you need something." Harper, a tenured faculty, agreed by sharing a positive experience she had in her workplace regarding clear expectations: "I think that they did a pretty good job of just very clearly articu-lating what the expectations were [for tenure] and that's good mentoring also." Participants discussed clear expectations for tenure as being essential to avoiding time spent doing unnecessary work and stress around the ambiguity of what will lead to success. Evelyn stated:

> So I think with respect to a healthy workplace, I think mental health, my mental health would be [laughter] much better if I knew more specifically what was required of me, after the, you know, three year, six year, in the milestone marks. That's—, that's been a key, primary issue for me. I think if that was well established and documented, everything else I can deal with because those are just a natural part of any working environment.

Brief Recommendations Toward a Healthy Environment All participants shared recommendations for what they felt would contribute to a healthy environment—the majority of these recommendations focused on creating safe spaces and allowing for open communication. These recommendations were primarily provided to deans and chairs of academic departments but also were useful for incoming students to take note of and to ask for advice from their supervisors. Isabella stated: "I think providing that safe place where you honestly can talk about your fears without having retaliation, that's the word. I think that is necessary. That is completely necessary." Charlotte stated that a "good environment consists of rigorousness in the field you're at as well as trying to communicate well your ideas without taking any experiences in the negative way." There is a clear emphasis on being able to speak freely without fear of retaliation from those in positions of power.

Support Groups Four participants recommended setting up support groups for women to promote conversations around struggles, best practices, and ways to survive and thrive in their academic spaces. Amelia's advice to deans and chairs included, "Informal or formal groups of female faculty that we can exchange best practices or have something that's a little bit more structured to be able to have some of these conversations and talk through some of these issues." Isabella, a program director, agreed, stating:

> [Support groups] could provide the opportunity to be open, to talk about the fears, to talk about the barriers that faculties are having. Providing the opportunity in a very safe way. And I think that's the tricky part because if it's a new faculty, it's a faculty on a tenure track, that person's going to be afraid to talk. And I think providing a safe place, it's necessary.

Open and Free Communication with Senior Administration In addition to suggesting that universities offer support groups, participants felt that one-on-one conversations with senior administrators could provide important opportunities for junior faculty navigating new spaces and the tenure track. Evelyn advised a written or outlined template for deans and department chairs to follow in regular, assigned meetings:

> So I think it would be beneficial for department chairs and deans to maybe have an individual one-on-one, maybe annually or even first semester to kind of say, this is all the support we're supposed to be providing. Are you receiving this? And if not, why.

Evelyn further goes on to note that "doing that in a one-on-one is much better than a group because I think often in a group, you don't want to call out your department chair… because they're not doing their job. So I think it would be helpful if deans and department chairs or administration would intentionally seek out those conversations to use self-assessment to understand how are we doing. Are we doing what we say we're going to do? And if not, what can be done?" In Evelyn's mind, the one-on-one conversations would be a safe place to share struggles and adversities and also receive necessary support to succeed. Charlotte agreed, describing the importance of encouraging conversations across seniority levels in departments that would assist in identifying barriers and structures that prevent women from succeeding: "Maybe have more conversations with the students and the post docs and even the faculty, like honest conversations. And try to have more workshops or more events, more discussion around those that will hopefully allow for some modifications." Olivia, a tenured faculty member, also offered some advice to deans: "Be fair. Be equitable. You know. Be consistent. Mentor your chairs, you know. Don't leave them in the dark. Don't let them hang themselves." Olivia is speaking once again to the importance of transparency and sharing clearly what is expected in her role as department chair.

In sum, the participants focused their discussions on healthy environments around clear, transparent expectations and safe, supportive opportunities to be heard. The literature shows that structural, interpersonal, and identity-related challenges can be buffered by a sense of voice [3]. Institutions that want to retain and better understand the challenges faced by women in their departments should open their doors and invite women to participate in conversations around the policies and procedures that affect them.

References

1. Eagly, A. H., Wood, W., & Diekman, A. B. (2000). Social role theory of sex differences and similarities: A current appraisal. In *The developmental social psychology of gender* (pp. 123–174). Mahwah: Lawrence Erlbaum Associates Publishers.
2. Flam, F. (1991). Still a "chilly climate" for women? *Science, 252*(5013), 1604–1606. https://doi.org/10.1126/science.252.5013.1604.
3. Settles, I. H. (2014, October). *Women in STEM: Challenges and determinants of success and well-being.* American Psychological Association. https://www.apa.org/science/about/psa/2014/10/women-stem
4. Silbey, S. S. (2016, August 23). Why do so many women who study engineering leave the field? *Harvard Business Review.* https://hbr.org/2016/08/why-do-so-many-women-who-study-engineering-leave-the-field
5. Walton, G. M., Logel, C., Peach, J. M., Spencer, S. J., & Zanna, M. P. (2014). Two brief interventions to mitigate a "chilly climate" transform women's experience, relationships, and achievement in engineering. *Journal of Educational Psychology, 107*(2), 468. https://doi.org/10.1037/a0037461.

Chapter 7
"Be Strong!" The Role of Self-Advocacy

In navigating the various challenges of being a STEM scientist in academia, a key theme for all participants was self-advocacy, the ability to advocate on behalf of oneself. Self-advocacy was expressed in several different ways: as a personal quality that participants ascribed to themselves as critical in overcoming obstacles; as a reflection of their choice of work setting, in terms of ensuring the site was a good fit for participants; and as a driving force in seeking out support from others.

Self-Advocacy as a Personal Quality

Many participants referred to their image or concept of themselves as being strong and willing to fight for what they wanted to be or do. Olivia, an African American woman working in a Historically Black College/University (HBCU), described herself as a "go-getter": "I'm a go-getter. I guess, you know, people are used to doing nothing and being told what to do. I'm the complete opposite. I'm a go-getter." This quality became particularly important for Olivia as she navigated a system that was highly competitive and at times dysfunctional, in which Olivia felt under intense scrutiny by her faculty peers as well as the administration, including visits during class by the dean. Olivia's response to being pressured to leave the university was "I am not going to let them harass me" and "I'm stronger than that... I have kids. I have bills to pay."

Similarly Ava, when she was a graduate student, observed her advisor was attempting to slow her graduation from the program as she neared completion, an all-too-common practice by university professors as students become highly skilled in their abilities:

> my boss didn't want me to graduate and leave and so again, things like writing our paper, which is a prerequisite of graduation. The paper sort of sat on his desk for a while before it

got reviewed. And luckily, because I wanted to apply for a policy fellowship and there was a…deadline, you know, I was able to exert some pressure to make sure that I was done by that time. I was able to sort of gather the support of my committee and other advocates at the university to make sure that I hit that deadline.

Isabela is a Latina professor who left her first academic position in a university in the Midwest because of openly anti-Latinx attitudes and remained unbowed about her future career: "I don't know if they actually block my path. I, I consider myself very strong." She continued to see herself as having "the personality to never say no and kind of open my own doors, never close doors." Her advice to students was similarly sage in urging them to not "let anybody, anybody, to put their feet on-, over them. So to be strong" as well as to focus on their respective abilities:

I really encourage my students to understand their strengths. Because they are bringing to the table so many other things that other students don't have. And, and those are the things that we need to actually do to … highlight all the strengths that people from different races and ethnicities…have.

Other participants emphasized self-advocacy as simply persisting through challenges, as Harper stated: "For me, it was just kind of keeping my eyes on what the goal was." Amelia similarly observed "I kind of tried to silence the doubt in my brain and just kept moving forward and saying, well, at some point, it's not going to work if I don't try. So I'm just going to keep at it."

Self-Advocacy in Career Decisions

Many participants engaged in self-advocacy strategies in decisions they made about where to work, as well as the type and structure of their work. For example, Isabella who experienced a hostile, anti-Latinx environment in her first academic position made the difficult decision to leave and seek a position in another placement, moving her entire family to a different state as a result:

I think making the decision to leave that very nasty environment it actually helped my path. It would have been horrible if I didn't notice the hostile environment that I was in and staying there for ten-, 15 years. So I think, right now I can appreciate those people for being very nasty. [laughter] Because I escaped that, that environment.

Charlotte consciously set out to identify work settings that emphasized support and resources rather than the prestige and power generally emphasized for academic positions: "So because I think my best potential in this is an environment that although has fantastic research, I wouldn't thrive in there because I would have to [laughter] associate and be part of a group. So I did not want go into that environment." P10 who had a great deal of research and grant writing experiences also sought to choose well in work place settings:

At all the places that I've been because I, you know, sought out institutions that I thought would be most helpful in that regard. And in particular, just making sure that there were other faculty that I could collaborate with that how into my journey development and then also other things that helped, basically resources. I will say that this is a common thing to making sure that the university that I went to had the right type of resources for me...You know, to make sure that I'm continuing to grow.

Sophia similarly focused on obtaining a position that would allow her to teach, conduct research, and engage in clinical practice, all while raising a family, by going a more nontraditional route without tenure pressures: "I was, you know, somewhat frantic at that point to actually get a position that I would, that I would feel good about. So I negotiated pretty hard for the position." Sophia was successful in doing so, now being in her 21st year of the position:

> And it's been incredibly comfortable... I found a way eventually to have a private practice, to teach, to train the next generation of clinicians, and to do research that is interesting and meaningful to me... And I have run multiple clinical trials. I have developed new treatments. I have done... research. And I do it all without a lick of funding...Ironically, because research productivity is not actually part of my job description, I also don't have to worry about the impact factor, the journals that I publish in...I can just do research that is truly interesting and engaging to me.

Sophia also advocated for herself regarding unfair expectations that she engages in unpaid work:

> There were other senior faculty in the department who were exploitative and expected me to take on burdens that were not part of my job description and to mentor undergraduate honor students and so on, with no extra compensation. I had to really fight to be appropriately compensated for the work that I was doing.

As a result of standing up for being compensated, Sophia now teaches an undergraduate research that incorporates mentorship:

> So my undergraduate research class actually was the result of my fight for that...Where a senior guy in the department who was director of undergraduate studies looked at me when I objected [to mentoring undergraduates]... I said: Look. I'm not being paid to mentor undergraduates. And he said: Well, doesn't the faculty get paid to mentor undergraduate honor students? I looked at him and I said: That is absolutely not true. Of course you get paid for that. You get paid with promotion and recognition and tenure and, and, and—And I'm not eligible for any of those things. So it is exploitative for you to expect me to take that on when I'm getting paid a quarter of what a tenure track faculty in my position would be being paid...I said: the only way I'm going to do it is if you find a way to compensate me appropriately.

Self-Advocacy in Seeking Support

As detailed in the chapter on seeking support, all participants sought various kinds of support as a means of achieving success. Many participants couched this strategy as a type of self-advocacy. For example, Emma stated, "I built my own support system that way by peers, therapy, and...reading literature that helped me get through it all." Charlotte also acknowledged that seeking support was a conscious strategy for surviving and thriving in the academy: "I'm good at realizing who's going to help me and who's like really interested in promoting my, my career... so when I met the head of the department, the head of the graduate program, ...I just knew that this person could be like a very good mentor for me. And I gravitated towards that." As Evelyn noted:

> In many cases, I also think I had to do a lot of the advocating on behalf of myself, and it could be, you know, drafting a letter of support that then I would go to a mentor to have them sign. And so I don't think that advocacy is like a sole person on their own. I think I played some part in trying to develop mentors or obtain advocacy.

Seeking particular types of mentors also was a self-advocacy strategy. For example, Evelyn highlighted the critical role that older or more experienced women in particular played as mentors, particularly as she sought support while being gaslighted to quit by her department chair: "I try to seek out women, experienced women, from different backgrounds and different locations within not only my institution but outside, just to kind of get in those different perspectives." Similarly Amelia pointed to the important role female mentors played regarding traditional gender roles, such as being a mother of school-aged children: "I kind of watch what she goes through with having three kids in high school and kind of she's super, super, super busy."

Chapter 8
Navigating "Mars": Resisting Structural Barriers in Academia

In July 2020, Congresswoman Alexandria Ocasio-Cortez (AOC) delivered a historic address regarding the general negative treatment of women in the workplace. The speech arose as a result of being called a misogynistic epithet by a fellow Congressman that AOC demanded be entered into the record. In particular, AOC was incensed about a woefully inadequate attempt at an apology by the Congressman, which some suggested reflected a typical "nonapology" offered by offenders regarding their harassing speech and behaviors toward women. In a speech heard by millions, AOC called out the reality of misogyny that women daily endure, particularly for those engaged in nontraditional gender roles, such as being a congressional representative or a scientist in academia.

Nearly all participants in the study expressed strong concerns about hostile treatment they received as women working in academic spaces. First, participants acknowledged the pain and uncertainty of navigating the academic environment found in many university departments in STEM disciplines that reflect an "old guard" mentality. Participants further described their brutalizing experiences during the hiring and tenure processes, how the scientific work itself was assigned or taught in laboratories and departments, and their experiences of microaggressions.

The Academic Environment as "Old Guard"

Many of the participants spoke of a general sense of academia as a male-dominant, particularly White male-dominant, atmosphere with little room to welcome, let alone successfully orient, newly minted doctoral-level women scientists. As Ava described, "One of the biggest impediments is just the fact that there's an old guard. And even sort of a younger generation of faculty and of scientists that are a little bit less interested in including everyone. They're maybe more competitive. There's more sort of an insular nature." The old guard was experienced quite visibly and palpably by Ava: "There's like a group of old men that sit in the front row. And they drive the conversation [at conferences and seminars], and they come every year."

Emma described parallel incidences that poignantly highlighted the negative impact of patriarchal attitudes and behaviors:

> So it was seminars that were being given by two women of color...One was an African American and one was Hispanic. And in both times, and yes, they were both, they were white men, both times. They—, during the conf-, during this pers-, these people [female presenters] giving their seminars, they [men in audience] were just having conversations with the person next to them. So [the men spoke] loud, where people would turn around and look at this person: What are you doing? ...When the sem-, with it was over, they essentially asked questions in very, almost aggressive manners. And they often repeated things that were-, that the presenter said in the seminar. But they were discussing it as if it was the first time that it was being said, as if they were teaching it to everyone else."

Emma further noted that in light of university initiatives promoting greater inclusiveness for women and people of color, there has been even further entrenchment of negative attitudes and continued lack of empathy for women: "My perception is that men-, and I guess in particular White men—think that women have it easy now... because there are greater pushes to increase women in STEM."

Ava similarly described a personally negative experience as a student presenting her research at a professional conference:

> I gave a talk at the super insular conference. And the first question I got was your results disagree with my results. And so they must be wrong...That was not a particularly welcoming feeling for a graduate student in her third or fourth year presenting her results for the first time. So he was very confident and I think that sort of competitive nature and the aggressive nature...on the surface it looks like it's about the science. But it sometimes feels like it's a more personal attack.

As Isabella who is Latina described, these attacks can take a racialized tone as well:

> When you have a chair from your own department laughing at you in your face because of your accent, that was pretty bad. And that was the moment that I said, you know what? This is not a good environment.... And now I realize that that environment is not okay for your productivity. You're not, you're not creating anything because you're just having all these nasty and very hostile environments around you.

Isabella further observed these attitudes remain deeply entrenched: "some people, males,...with a very strong, I don't know how to say it, like a macho role, you know. That sometimes that still exists in that kind of senior males that they usually try to prevent having women around because historically they haven't had many women around."

Negative experiences in even how participants were identified in their department directory further reflected hostile attitudes toward women, as seen in Sophia's anecdote from early in her time in her department:

> They put up a new department directory near the front door of our major buildings. And there was a man who was on tenure track, who was like a research assistant professor or something like that, who was listed with all the standing faculty. And then there were three

of us who were women non-tenured track faculty who, interestingly enough, were listed with the administrative staff.

In response, Sophia engaged in self-advocacy strategies:

And I saw that and went to my chair and said, this is, number one, ridiculous because no student coming to look for us is going to think to look under, you know, with the secretaries. And number two, it's insulting and inappropriate and sexist and it has to get changed….To his credit, the chair didn't necessarily acknowledge that it had been done intentionally or anything. But agree to have the directory remade. And to have the women faculty listed with the faculty rather than with the secretaries.

Amelia also described the pervasive, even unspoken nature of how women simply are not welcomed in STEM disciplines in academia: "When I transitioned to a faculty position, I really had no idea of all of the under the surface stuff that would be happening… and something that is subtle and nuanced, in some ways, and in other ways blatant and not subtle at all." And further: "all these other unspoken processes are actually happening, and…the people who are in leadership positions at in my, in my program, in my department, in my college, I don't think they really see that…All of them are White males, and I'm not sure that they get it."

At the same time, Amelia, along with several others, acknowledged the positive contributions that individual men had on their careers, as helpful mentors or academic leaders, and then attempting to align this fact within the context of an unmistakably hostile environment:

That's why this is so confusing… on one hand, how can I feel so supported by all these individuals and yet feel like the system is just upside down…it's such a powerful force to keep things the way they are…and to not really have a place for my voice to be heard. How can both of those be true at the same time?

Evelyn similarly tried to make sense of her department chair, using a familiar Venus/Mars dichotomy from the popular media:

Because I currently have a male department chair and often [laughter] I don't always get what he's trying to accomplish. Or even in conversations, I don't understand his thought process…this is just reality. Men and women are different. You know, men are from Mars, women are from Venus. So trying to understand those underlying messages, what's really going on?

Evelyn observed how this dichotomy harms women in particular:

So I think that's something that impacts women much more than men because women probably tend to overthink and are more relationship focused…When I was going through this process with this department chair [being gaslighted with scare tactics to quit her position], I—, while I was sitting there, I thought: He would never do this to a man, to say 'go back and think about it, maybe go meet with HR to figure out what your options are.' So I think that experience was intentional for women. I don't think he would have done that same thing to a man.

As a result of these negative work experiences, Evelyn strategized by responding with traditional masculine forms of behavior:

And so I've been trying to be more intentional about writing more, I guess, masculine oriented emails and even when I draft memos. I've read articles that say: Men want you to go straight to the point at the beginning, vs. having this whole long narrative and making the point at the end. So I've been more intentional when I write emails or draft memos that are a primary audience of men. I try to follow many of those rules because if that's—. Men are from Mars. Women are from Venus. I'll try to—to me that means I can increase the communication.

Hiring and Tenure Process

Structural barriers were also reflected in the processes of hiring and becoming tenured in the academy. As an African American woman working in an HBCU, Olivia described multiple experiences of sabotage and retaliation by colleagues:

> It was an all male department for the majority, I would say, 90% international faculty. And as a Black woman in that position [department chair]... not only that, my faculty was mostly Muslim and I was, I'm a Christian woman. And I know at least one in particular had a problem with that, you know?...And I thought that was so wrong that they allowed him to retaliate against me once I had written him up...No penalty. Nothing.

The retention and rewarding of male professors with tenure despite problematic behaviors with women also was noted by Charlotte: "And he also had problems with other students... it shouldn't be appropriate...After many students spoke up, he was investigated...but he still obtained tenure."

In contrast, women's experiences after hiring were often nullifying and isolating. Amelia described an egregious approach to her orientation by the department:

> I think one of the roadblocks I came to work every day and sometimes I wouldn't see a single other person. And so I kind of didn't know how to navigate the system like I didn't know where I was supposed to be like the first day. I didn't know we had an administrator for our department and an administrative assistant until three months in, that I didn't know this person existed or the first faculty meeting they forgot to tell me about. And so I didn't go.

Amelia's orientation to her new position was so poor that "I was locked out of my office four times before I realized all the different sets of keys and pass codes and swipe cards I needed like that kind of stuff." Understandably, Amelia's reaction was to question her own sanity and fitness for the setting: "[you] think you're losing your mind at some point, like, what, what am I doing, I can't get into my office. I don't know who to ask for support. I mean by support, I mean, like, a key."

As Emma wryly observed:

> I come from a lower socioeconomic status. I'm a woman. I'm a woman of color. These systems were not built for me to be in and to thrive in... Recognizing that there's nothing wrong with me per se, it's that I've been invited to a party where no one told me what the rules were.

Evelyn shared a particular brutal incident regarding her current position status:

> And so what this new department chair was trying to do was get me to quit on my own so that this didn't have to be a problem with other departments, to have to take me in and fit me in as a budget line item. So his approach, which is unfortunate, is to try to gaslight me,

to try to quit, and put in some scare tactics and requiring me to go meet with HR… And this is where it's been helpful to talk to another administrator and helpful to talk to more experienced tenured faculty because this isn't new. These tactics are not new.

Evelyn further reflected on the more troubling aspects of gender and the tenure process:

> So I think the prevention [of career advancement of women] is the P&T, the promotion and tenure process and the subjectivity around it. Because then knowing that men are from Mars and women are from Venus, and men get along better with other men and vice versa, women get along better with other women. And knowing that the decision makers are primarily men, I think that's a prevention. So the subjectivity of the promotion and tenure process.

Amelia reflected on her ambivalence about learning to act like a man in academia as a means of successfully penetrating the "old guard" space:

> Negotiating like a man is kind of what you get if that's what you want. On the other hand, I, I feel slimy to even say that. We're not men, and we don't need to act like men, but that's how the structure is set up… it was so eye opening and so being able to match…our behavior with what's valued at the university, which is not necessarily what we as women come in with.

Sophia similarly had reflections about the gender-based nature of tenure and even sabbatical policies:

> Don't allow male faculty to get away with using parental leave as a sabbatical… And then don't come back and look at women and say: Oh, well. You know, yeah, they stopped the tenure clock but we're still actually going to evaluate them based on seven years of potential productivity rather than six.

The Work of Science

Participants also reflected on gender-based barriers they encountered while learning about the work of science as students and then pursuing their careers as STEM scientists in academia. For example, Ava spoke about the notion of "office housework" in how work within a laboratory typically was divided among students:

> In grad school a lot of the time… we were, particularly women, sort of shifted into the planner category, or like the assistant category… we kept the calendar. We made sure that lunch was ordered. And, you know, we planned parties.

Ava observed the eventual negative outcome of doing all the office housework: "But then when you're organizing something for like the 13th time, you're no longer gaining skills." Charlotte similarly described the "toxic environment" in her graduate program that attempted to harness her skills without providing any support, training, or mentoring:

> It was just hostile. …One of the reasons that I've been able to be successful in my career is because I am a good scientist…I ask the right questions. I learn very fast.…So in my experience…a young investigator [who was her first advisor] saw that potential and just took

advantage of it…He wanted just me to be his technician as opposed to actually teaching me and mentoring me.

Emma described a toxically competitive environment from lead or principal investigators (PI) regarding collaborations for grant writing and the lack of mentoring: "There were no discussions about expectations. There were no discussions about what I would need to do, what I should expect my PI to do. And so there was a lot of …being lost for a lot of time and just sort of figuring it out." Emma further decried "the lack of transparency. The lack of ability to just talk about what's going on… I didn't feel comfortable talking to him [principal investigator]… he wasn't like a bad person. He just was not very communicatory." Unfortunately given the lack of communication, the potential for training was lost: "that kind of culture that's get bred with that…if the PI is not communicatory, the students don't learn."

Wasted time also was part of the process for Emma, putting her professional development and potential for success at risk, and worse, with her ideas being taken without proper attribution: "I would have scientific ideas, talk them with my PI, get little feedback on whether or not they were good. But then I'd hear that…those ideas that I had talked about were being done by someone. And I was like, wait a minute, like I talked about that with him."

Emma described the negative psychological impact that resulted on her self-concept as a young scientist, leading perhaps to the development of an imposter syndrome:

Like that's the thing I wanted to do and now it's being done somewhere else. And I, and I have no idea why. And, so then of course I would internalize that and say: Well, you know, maybe either he-, they just didn't want to work with me. Or, you know, they didn't think I would do a good job at it? Like I had a good idea, but they didn't trust me enough to do it.

Toxically competitive behaviors also had negative impact on early career professionals in terms of isolation, as observed by Charlotte:

Right now, I'm at a senior level. And I have done really, really well…So that kind of isolates you in the sense that people do not—, don't like—. It seems like they don't want to help. So yes, right now we're writing a grant with my PI, and there's supposed to be three people writing the grant. But since it's focused on expanding my project for the lab, yeah, I'm basically doing it myself.

Microaggressions Another kind of barrier that women may encounter in academia is microaggressions. However, despite the awareness of the gender-based hostility that most participants described both in graduate school and throughout their careers, almost no participant was able to identify and discuss specific microaggressions. Emma's description is typical: "I guess my experience with microaggressions is I usually talk myself out of the fact that I might have just had one." Emma further described:

I usually internalize it and say it's my fault. And I think that's maybe just how I was raised or just my own previous experiences. I, I've not turned around and said: This person is, you know, being this way to me and that's not cool. Like it's usually like: Oh, did I just imagine that? You know. That didn't really happen. Like they're really cool. Like they wouldn't say

that, they wouldn't do that. Like that's not—if something happened, I'm just misunderstanding the situation.

Ultimately, Emma acknowledged that naming microaggressions may just be too
painful and aggravating to do: "I think I've trained myself really well to just ignore
that kind of thing…Because if I actually paid attention to it and I told myself that it
really did happen and it was real, I think I would just be pissed off all the time."

Chapter 9
Discussion of Findings

We interviewed ten women who were trained as doctoral-level scientists in a variety of STEM fields (e.g., biology, microbiology, computer science, clinical psychology, and rehabilitation sciences). As we saw in the previous chapters, these participants shared poignantly of their experiences working in the academic setting. Per our analyses, we found several themes reflected in these narratives: finding and developing support systems, particularly mentors, peers, and spouses, the last of whom were critical for personal decision-making regarding having children; healthy vs. unhealthy work environments; navigating structural barriers that long have been a part of academic settings; and self-advocacy. In this chapter, we discuss these findings in the context of the available literature to provide a more comprehensive understanding. First, we will discuss each set of results per the four themes and then briefly consider the overall meaning of these findings. The final chapter of the book will describe the implications of the findings for individuals and leaders in organizational contexts.

The Role of Support Without a doubt, a critical finding that facilitated success and satisfaction for all the participants was the role of supportive people in their personal lives and at work. All participants described mentors as particularly crucial at every point of their careers. In the chapter on Support, we described Kram's [11] scholarship on mentors' career and psychosocial functions. When participants were students, mentors were critical in teaching the basic components of science as well as how to network and meet others within the field. For both students and professionals, mentors also served as critical information and emotional support sources who assisted in the survival of participants, especially in more hostile circumstances. These findings provide further evidence that the overall career development of women scientists can be enhanced through effective mentoring, which has long been linked to performance, success, and career advancement [10]. Participants further spoke to the importance of a mentoring relationship that was transparent and

© The Author(s), under exclusive license to Springer Nature Switzerland AG 2022
P. Arredondo et al., *Women and the Challenge of STEM Professions*, International and Cultural Psychology, https://doi.org/10.1007/978-3-030-62201-5_9

genuine and showed interest in their personal goals and growth. Recent research examining woman-to-woman mentoring relationships for tenure-track faculty found that the holistic relationships (involving advice/guidance, honesty, and listening well) helped women faculty navigate the tenure process more effectively [13].

A unique contribution of mentoring for participants seemed to reflect the work of Belenky et al. [5] who described women's unique ways of knowing including silence, received knowledge, listening to the voices of others, subjective knowledge or the inner voice, procedural knowledge: separate and connected knowing, and constructed knowing: integrating the voices. Each of these kinds of ways, especially listening to and integrating the voices of others, may be relevant to the impact of mentors for participants as women reflected in their general learning and overall progress, gave voice to others who experienced similar challenges, connected the dots when it came to making sense of difficult or opaque work situations, and balanced multiple and differing perspectives, for example, seeking and obtaining tenure. Mentoring also attenuated some of the negative impacts of participants' experiences of imposter syndrome and their sense of being presumed incompetent, especially for women of color, by providing clear affirmation of their abilities and potential as well as participants' critique of their unsupportive work settings. Mentoring was provided in the context of resonant leadership to several participants, helping to prolong more positive emotions in difficult times and situations through encouraging and attentive behavior [3, 4].

In addition to mentors, finding support in others sharing or doing similar work was important to participants' survival and success. Beginning during student days, participants benefitted when sharing their experiences first in changing the ways work responsibilities in a laboratory were distributed so that the gender disparity of women doing more of the "office housework" was actually changed. Peer support remained important as participants advanced in their careers, especially as women encountered hostile or opaque work circumstances. Some participants specifically became engaged in organizations and programs emphasizing diversity, equity, inclusion, and access (DEIA) initiatives designed to assist them in succeeding in their departments and universities. These organizations and programs provided important analyses about the lack of diversity in STEM climates, thus providing normalization and relief regarding their struggles with colleagues or administrators that several participants had experienced (e.g., being the target of scare tactics).

Finally, supportive people in participants' personal lives proved crucial in facilitating decision-making about beginning a family. Indeed participants who chose to have children clearly identified their spouse as absolutely critical to the decision, especially spouses who gave up their own career goals to help ensure participants' success in their faculty jobs. Having a supportive spouse was essential to combating the "baby penalty" that women typically face, especially in the academic setting, when tenure demands and raising families co-occur at the same time.

Work Environments Participants provided poignant accounts of their multiple experiences with unsupportive environments, especially regarding communications from administrators about proper orientation to their role and settings and work assignments. As described earlier, clearly, many of the participants were making their way through a labyrinth that often placed them in second-class positions. Learning to navigate an opaque climate, where expectations and clear directions are not provided readily, was tremendously frustrating to participants. Moreover, when participants were attended to or given responsibilities by their advisors or administrators, these often had the flavor of an "assistant" role, rather than as an apprentice or cherished mentee. Some participants further felt they were asked to "serve" the institution by taking on extra work without discussion of extra pay, leaving participants to feel demoralized and out of place. Those inviting them to take on more responsibilities had positional power, rendering individuals unable to say "no" to the request or assignment.

The impact of multiple identities, as in the case of women of color, who made up half of our participant pool, is relevant. That is, academic environments are even "chillier" for individuals who come from multiple marginalized group experiences, per gender and race/ethnicity, who may feel that much more isolated and alienated as a result. Networking with supportive and knowledgeable others and becoming engaged with programs and organizations that affirm the rights and experiences of women of color in academic settings help ensure the survival and success of these women.

As a result of these experiences, participants provided several excellent suggestions on how to improve these work environments. For example, they suggested that universities train administrators (deans and department chairs) on how to engage in open communication and regularly check in with faculty, particularly new faculty, as to their experiences beyond simply publishing outcomes. Moreover, participants suggested that support groups be created so that individuals can share openly with each other without fear of retaliation.

Navigating "Mars" Participants also shared about their experiences navigating gender-based structural barriers. For example, the Matilda effect (being given no credit for their work) was at play for both students and professionals. Women described sharing ideas with a senior mentor or colleague who provided no initial positive feedback and then learned later that someone else was moving forward with their idea. Such experiences were coupled with resultant self-doubt or a sense of impostorism, as women struggled to make sense of these behaviors toward them by others. Being "otherized," women felt themselves as outsiders, to the point of regularly being made to feel unwelcome. As one participant had described in her initial days in her department, no one, including the department chair, bothered to inform her about the first department meeting, which she missed as a result. A palpable sense of the "old guard" and criticisms that masked personal attacks were frequent for participants as they engaged in professional presentations of their work. As our results demonstrate, many STEM academic units, unfortunately, remain male-designed systems and structures where traditional forms of power and privilege are manifested, isolating women, and leading them to continue experiencing a "chilly climate." Such climates only further exacerbated any feelings of stereotype threat or imposter syndrome, rather than effectively combating and changing these cognitive distortions and negative self-perceptions.

Issues of positionality also were of concern, with power and privilege being readily ascribed to White men in the university system, leaving participants to feel invisible as to the significance of their roles (e.g., being listed as administrative staff versus part of the faculty). Harding's standpoint theory [6] is relevant here. The pyramid model of social hierarchies makes up higher education, with the scholars at the top who are mostly White men. They are simply unable to perceive, let alone, appreciate, and effectively respond to the unique experiences of those further down the hierarchy, ignoring the multiple social realities they do not live. It is almost no wonder that women have the isolating, alienating experiences they shared with us.

Further complicating the Martian landscape is navigating the combined impact of race and ethnicity with gender as a woman of color. Being presumed incompetent was a common experience for many participants, for example, when working with an advisor whose presumed role was as educator and mentor, but whose actual role was revealed to be as harasser or, worse, thief of women's unique ideas and perspectives. Utilizing Arredondo's Dimensions of Identity model [1] which highlights the complexities of women's visible, invisible, and intersecting identities as well as Crenshaw's [7] call to understand better intersectionality in the lives of women of color, the particular experiences of STEM scientists from these backgrounds are more clearly understood. Attributions based on visible identities, family status, age, and domestic versus international cultural heritage are but a few examples of characteristics that are out of a woman's control. Yet, negative assumptions and attributions persisted regarding these aspects of self, as several participants shared. One Latina participant even left a highly desired faculty position because of the open condescension regarding her accent expressed by her department chair to her. As a result of such microaggressions, women of color experienced continuous challenges to their self-esteem and self-efficacy, as well as a pervasive sense of the precarious nature of their position, which ultimately reflected their status, power, and privilege within their institutions.

Gender and racial-ethnic positionality complicated promotion and tenure (P&T) processes, leaving some participants to wonder whether P&T was simply another structured way of stopping women's advancement in science and academia. Tannen [15, 16] cites how men use their positionality in workplace situations to silence women and attempt to reduce or disqualify or take their perspectives; participant narratives confirmed these persistent experiences. Male faculty with questionable interpersonal behaviors were retained under the sometimes murky circumstances surrounding P&T procedures and final decisions. In contrast, hardworking female faculty without such behaviors were let go, served to confirm participants' suspicions as to the "objective" (i.e., male-centered) nature of P&T.

Historic racial and gender stereotypes and values led to a lack of orientation and communication practices that left participants feeling either targeted or diminished, though happily at the point of interviews, all participants continued to persist in their academic positions. These work practices speak to stereotypes and presumed incompetence of women as not possessing qualities to work independently and lead and supervise. Participant narratives regarding the precariousness of their positions also supported previous findings of the harsh realities of needing to engage in diplomacy, mistrust, and hypervigilance as means of survival and success [2].

Self-Advocacy Our final set of findings center on women's sense of agency and self-efficacy as they make their way through and negotiate the academic environment. The ability to advocate for oneself was a hallmark of women scientists who succeeded in their goals to achieve their education and careers. One way to understand this set of findings is through a "sense of agency," an individual's cognitive thought process about what she believes she can do and can actually do [8]. Others have talked about the agency as behavior, demonstrating that one assumes responsibility and influences one's own life [12]. In doing so, individuals are also developing resilience to manage challenging and stressful situations, both personally and professionally. By so doing, women grow in self-respect. Participants expressed self-advocacy in several ways. For example, as a personal quality, they attributed to themselves that they turned to in especially challenging times and as conscious strategies that led to seeking supportive others and work environments.

Speaking up on one's behalf comes with some risks, especially in chilly climates. Eagly and Chin [9] reported that women of color often receive even less affirming feedback about their intellectual talent than their White counterparts. These double standards for women of color introduce a double bind. Women, in general, have been socialized to not self-promote, but when a woman of color has no advocates, she experiences isolation and self-doubt about her competencies. However, as the participants indicated, she may have to make the difficult decision to engage in self-advocacy and risk the possibility that others will see her as a braggart. Retribution for speaking up may lead to stigma, the disapproval of a person because she has stepped out of her expected gendered role, leading to further isolation and pressures. Another perception of a self-assured woman is that of role congruence violations [14, 17]. If women are expected to remain silent and follow a man's lead, speaking up may be viewed unfavorably. In contrast, as some participants indicated, they also may learn to "act like a man" leading to some success in, for example, job or contract negotiations, but with a resultant distaste toward oneself about having to resort to such accommodating practices. An inadvertent result may be that institutions of higher education and science itself are robbed of unique perspectives and practices that women, including women of color, bring to these situations.

On a positive note, knowing how to advocate for oneself also may help establish one's mentoring approach. Success through self-advocacy and mindful choices of strategies helps socialize mentees' focus on their strengths and unique assets and perspectives. They also may learn to navigate the difficult waters of STEM science and academic settings.

Limitations

As a qualitative study, our project focused on an in-depth exploration of the experiences of a smaller number of participants (10) rather than collecting data from a large number of participants, using convenience and snowball sampling techniques. Thus limitations regarding small nonrandom samples are relevant here, such as the applicability of our findings beyond our sample. However, although our sample size was limited, even within this sample, we collected data to the point of saturation, that is, until we felt participant narratives were reflecting each other in substantive ways. Future research might utilize quantitative approaches with larger numbers of participants, for example, exploring relevant variables, including organizational climate, experiences with sexism or microaggressions, and changes in self-efficacy as a result of positive or negative experiences in the academy, to further investigate women's experiences in STEM sciences in the academy.

Another study limitation involves the settings from which participants were drawn. Although our sample was quite racially and ethnically diverse (50% were women of color), nearly all (8 of 10) participants solely had worked in predominantly White institutions (PWI). In contrast, one participant worked at an HBCU, and another participant had briefly (and happily) worked in a tribal college. Also, the majority had earned their doctoral degree in a Research 1 university. Thus, future research might explore women's experiences across academic settings to better understand the unique roles that type of institution might play in women's experiences. Finally, since the sample pool included self-identified cisgender women, the experiences of transgender and gender-nonconforming individuals in STEM academic settings must still be explored.

Summary and Conclusions

As we consider the meaning of our findings as a whole, we find our participants' shared narratives to support much of the literature regarding women's career development, institutional barriers, and individual and organizational strategies for change. Although these will be addressed more comprehensively in the final chapter of the book, we provide a brief analysis.

As can be seen in the self-advocacy section, women scientists who have positive beliefs about themselves as strong individuals able to mount "the good fight" in support of their disciplinary and career goals are advantaged in hostile work environments that were built to ensure others' success, rather than their own. Part of mounting a fight for many participants was to mindfully select settings they felt would support them through the availability of people and resources they felt were critical to their success. Others who inadvertently found themselves amid a hostile work environment, including settings that seemed actively to oust them, sought out supportive people within and beyond their environments. This was for both emotional support and information that would promote their ultimate survival. Managing self-perceptions and strategies for success and survival were critical to combating attributions, labeling, and titling that reflected negative male-centric meanings in universities. Seeing oneself as strong to begin with or strong as a result of successfully solving difficult work setting problems likely helped women internalize more positive and capable images of themselves than what they were being socialized to believe as female students and early career professionals.

As a result of their successes, women develop piercing critiques and concomitant wisdom that, if attended to by university administrators and leading scientific organizations, can uncouple race and gender characteristics from success, learning, and advancing scientific knowledge to ever-expanding audiences. Doing so will further the advancement of both institutions of learning and science itself by integrating the unique perspectives and practices that women, including women of color, bring.

References

1. Arredondo, P. (1996). *Successful diversity management initiatives: A blueprint for planning and implementation.* Thousand Oaks: Sage.
2. Arredondo, P. (2011). The "borderlands" experience for women of color as higher education leaders. In J. L. Martin (Ed.), *Women as leaders in education: Succeeding despite inequity, discrimination, and other challenges* (pp. 275–298). Santa Barbara: Praeger Press.
3. Arredondo, P. (2018a). Latinx women aspiring, persisting, and maintaining cultural integrity. In P. A. Perez (Ed.), *The tenure-track process for Chicana and Latina faculty: Experiences of resisting and persisting in the academy* (pp. 106–129). London: Taylor & Francis.
4. Arredondo, P. (2018b). Thriving with optimism, purpose, and connectivity entre fronteras. In L. Comas-Diaz & C. I. Vazquez (Eds.), *The practice of Latina psychologists: Thriving in the cultural borderlands* (pp. 194–210). London: Taylor & Francis/Routledge.
5. Belenky, M. F., Clinchy, B. M., Goldberger, N., & Tarule, J. M. (Eds.). (1986). *Women's ways of knowing: The development of self, voice, and mind* (10th anniversary ed.). New York: Basic Books.
6. Borland, E. (2020). *Standpoint theory.* Encyclopedia Britannica. https://www.britannica.com/topic/standpoint-theory
7. Crenshaw, K. (*1989*). Demarginalizing the intersection of race and sex: A black feminist critique of antidiscrimination doctrine, feminist theory and antiracist politics. *University of Chicago Legal Forum, 1989*(1), 31.
8. Duggins, S. D. (2011). *The development of sense of agency* (Georgia State University). https://scholarworks.gsu.edu/psych_theses/88
9. Eagly, A. H., & Chin, J. L. (2010). Diversity and leadership in a changing world. *American Psychologist, 65*(3), 216–224. https://doi.org/10.1037/a0018957.
10. Hund, A. K., Churchill, A. C., Faist, A. M., Havrilla, C. A., Stowell, S. M. L., McCreery, H. F., Ng, J., Pinzone, C. A., & Scordato, E. S. C. (2018). Transforming mentorship in STEM by training scientists to be better leaders. *Ecology and Evolution, 8*(20), 9962–9974. https://doi.org/10.1002/ece3.4527.
11. Kram, K. E. (1986). Mentoring at work: Developmental relationships in organizational life. *Human Resource Management, 25*(4), 639–644. https://doi.org/10.1002/hrm.3930250410.
12. Lamia, M. C. (2010, October 15). Your sense of agency: Influencing your own life and taking responsibility. *Psychology Today.* http://www.psychologytoday.com/blog/the-white-knight-syndrome/201010/your-sense-agency-influencing-your-own-life-and-taking

13. Palmer, E. M., & Jones, S. J. (2019). Woman-woman mentoring relationships and their roles in tenure attainment. *Journal of Women and Gender in Higher Education, 12*(1), 1–17. https://doi.org/10.1080/19407882.2019.1568264.
14. Rosette, A. S., & Tost, L. P. (2010). Agentic women and communal leadership: How role prescriptions confer advantage to top women leaders. *Journal of Applied Psychology, 95*(2), 221–235. https://doi.org/10.1037/a0018204.
15. Tannen, D. (1990a). Gender differences in conversational coherence: Physical alignment and topical cohesion. In *Conversational organization and its development* (pp. 167–206). Norwood: Ablex Publishing.
16. Tannen, D. (1990b). *You just don't understand: Women and men in conversation.* New York: Harper Collins.
17. Toosi, N. R., Mor, S., Semnani-Azad, Z., Phillips, K. W., & Amanatullah, E. T. (2019). Who can lean in? The intersecting role of race and gender in negotiations. *Psychology of Women Quarterly, 43*(1), 7–21. https://doi.org/10.1177/0361684318800492.

Chapter 10
Recommendations and Commitments for Retaining STEM Women in the Academy

Addressing Culture and Climate Issues in the Academy

In her research on early women scientists, Rossiter (2019) identified several themes to describe exclusionary behavior that may still hold relevance today: "Absenting" women, male enclaves, absolutely "no" to women, "unprepared," and "not a good fit." Of course, she also coined the term "the Matilda effect" to signal the ways women are not given credit for their work. These themes continued to play out, as reported by participants in our study.

"Why do so many women who study engineering leave the field?" [22] described much of what we found in our study. According to Silbey, though women make up 20% of engineering graduates, 40% either leave the profession or simply never enter it. Her longitudinal study with colleagues of 700 engineering students began in 2003 [22]. They found that women were as well-prepared or even more prepared than were their male peers; however, it was the male-centric culture of engineering that drove women away. Among the negative experiences was working on teams. Often the men and male faculty would make them do secretarial and more menial tasks, while the men would do the real engineering work. We heard this in our study. The internship experience was another example from Silbey's report. Again, there was differential treatment by supervisors who sexually harassed the doctoral students and gave them paperwork to sort through while giving the men engineering assignments. According to Silbey's findings, women left the profession for two primary reasons—the lip service given by engineering to make a difference in society and the pervasive culture of sexism and stereotypes about women that were unaddressed.

Understanding the influence of climate and culture has become a priority for provosts, deans, and department chairs; after all, valuable resources are spent recruiting and hiring talented STEM women, but far too many leave before securing tenure. Instituting changes to retain women in the sciences and engineering requires

© The Author(s), under exclusive license to Springer Nature Switzerland AG 2022
P. Arredondo et al., *Women and the Challenge of STEM Professions*, International and Cultural Psychology, https://doi.org/10.1007/978-3-030-62201-5_10

a rationale that can be articulated and intentionality to follow through. The reasons are many, as we read in the Silbey accounting and throughout previous chapters. The forces of demographic change are one of the drivers for prioritizing the retention of STEM women, as is the revolving door reputation of institutions that seem to push out underrepresented students, faculty of color, and women faculty and administrators. Evidence of the chilly climate first discussed in [9] (Hall and Sandler) continues to be reported in contemporary literature and research studies. In *Presumed Incompetent II* [20], academic women of color contributors give voice to dynamics, behaviors, and institutional neglect that engender adverse consequences on career aspirations, health and mental health, and trust in others. This second edition, like the first book *Presumed Incompetent* [17], should be required reading for all administrators and faculty alike. Herein, they will learn about how bullying occurs, the liability of protecting faculty who demonstrate White fragility, how silent bias manifests, and the pervasiveness of microaggressions toward women. The 33 chapters in *Presumed Incompetent II* [20] are made up of powerful personal essays, as was the first edition. As with the research findings discussed in Chaps. 4 and 5 of this book, the narratives and examples are women's lived experiences.

For department chairs and deans in STEM programs with measurable goals for success based on faculty retention and promotion, articles published, grant dollars secured, nominations to the National Academies of Sciences, Engineering, and Medicine, and a high number of distinguished professors, there needs to be a roadmap and accountability about how women and women of color achieve these goals for their career advancement. As a consultant to university provosts and deans over the years (Arredondo) who indicate a desire to attend to women's retention and success, one of our first discussions is about motivation. I recall consulting with the dean of a large college of engineering in the West and questioning him about the college and departmental climate and culture. He seemed puzzled at first and then smiled and said, "This is a male bastion, but not for long." The year was 2003. In 2018, the same college of engineering had had two women deans, numerous women department chairs, and an increase in the enrollment of doctoral students of color, including women. Change can happen steadily with focus, commitment, and resources. Though I have not returned to conduct a climate study, I surmise that the culture has evolved and continues to change. I know that the university has an ADVANCE grant to provide mentorship, resources, and other assets for STEM women, but of course, the grant cannot change campus climate and culture; it is a matter of human resources and leadership.

Another recommendation for deans, chairs, and provosts is to make certain that men are part of the change processes. That is, if only women are brought together to recommend how the department can be friendlier and less chilly and to identify the effects of microaggressions in everyday relationships, the change will not occur. Men and women have to be part of this discussion together. I (Arredondo) recall a meeting of senior administrators who were presented with findings from a focus group of faculty women and administrators. The men were shocked to hear that women felt silenced, minimized, and disrespected. They simply never "noticed" this behavior in meetings or other university encounters as coming from them. Of note is the number of women needing to be in a unit for them to be a force amid systemic racism, sexism, and unconscious bias. Lack of a critical mass of Black women in predominantly White institutions keeps the bureaucracy intact [11].

A study by the Wellesley Center for Women found that the critical number for women's impact on a governance board is 3 [12]. Supreme Court Justice Ruth Bader Ginsburg illuminates the point in her statement about how litigators often mistook her for Justice O'Connor, the first female justice. With the addition of Justices Kagan and Sotomayor, confusion about who the two women—O'Connor and Ginsburg—unlikely would occur, she noted [13]. Department and college administrators should note not only the number of women scientists in their units but also how they are engaged, versus talked over, ignored, or, otherwise, objectified.

The construct of resistance was recently reconceptualized by Miville [14, 15] to emphasize its more positive, constructive aspects as an essential driver of social advocacy and change. Resistance to culture change for representation and inclusion thus should not be dismissed by leaders but understood for what it potentially contributes to the process of change. For example, resistance may be a response to the unfamiliar and unpredictable (woman scientist); a change in the department equilibrium because a new person has to be accommodated, a threat of loss to one's power and authority, and perceived as imposed versus agreed-upon change [4]. If unattended, resentment toward the newcomer may set in and render her powerless and a victim to an unhealthy environment. It is the responsibility of leaders to ensure that microaggressions and other manners of delegitimizing women cease and are dealt with immediately.

Policies for Hiring and Promotion and Tenure

Data previously reported in Chap. 1 points to the small percentage of STEM women graduates. The dropout from the profession before or upon graduation [22] means there is a small pipeline. The few available women will likely be selective about where they accept a position, and we recommend the following guidelines that can become policies:

- Have a blueprint that guides the recruitment to the hiring process that can be introduced to search committees.
- Prepare search committees to recognize unconscious biases. These relate to where a woman earned her terminal degree, her previous place of employment, her research agenda, her relationship or marital status, and other personal attributes that become visible during interviews. Remind search committee members that to say someone is "not a good fit" is not an acceptable rationale for not hiring.
- STEM women, according to interest inventories, typically demonstrated what is characterized as male interests and potentially masculine traits. Negative stereotypes about women scientists as being more "male-like" can be barriers to fairly evaluating any candidate who diverges from presumably traditional gender roles. It behooves search committees to openly discuss their biases about gender and

science, so they do not interfere during interviewing processes. International scholars who speak with an accent may be viewed less favorably as may individuals who are transgender or gender non-conforming. Though human resource policies are in place to protect individuals from discriminatory practices, personal biases often intrude.

- Policies about salaries and hiring packages are generally in place, but attention to salary equity is necessary so that the woman scientist is fairly compensated. Besides lab space and an office, start-up packages often include a stipend to be used over a 2-year period; a research associate; release time from teaching, particularly during the first semester; and a reduced teaching load perhaps for the first 2 years.
- Negotiations by women have often been criticized if it appears as though the woman is asking for more than a man would ask [27]. This is labeled role incongruity [7]. Another concern in the negotiation and hiring process is color blindness. Although most individuals will not openly make prejudicial or racist statements, to state one is "color blind" is a signal of bias [19].
- Retaining STEM women is possible with supportive and affirming practices as well as a "roadmap for retention." This is the administrators' responsibility, particularly the department chair who shares the roadmap with the woman scientist and all department faculty. The roadmap may include mentorship plans, introduction to senior campus administrators, informal presentations about one's research, recognition as appropriate, and inclusion on high-level college or institutional committees and task forces.
- The workload for women often runs them ragged [17, 20], and this can compromise evaluations for promotion and tenure generally based on excellent demonstration of research, teaching, and service. Although service is often not valued as highly, deans and department chairs need to note the number of committees women scientists are invited to serve on and the number of dissertation committees for which they are readers or chairs. It is often reported that women of color, particularly, are sought after by students of color. Though these students may have advisors, the cultural fit with a faculty of color is more affirming, although this may lead to more advising by women of color faculty. Also, concerning the faculty of color, there may be colleagues of color on campus they may connect with, especially if they are the only ones in their department. Chairs should not hold this against the woman scientist who also requires a sense of cultural validation and support.
- Work-life balance continues to be a challenge for women faculty. Testimony was provided in our study with women indicating that without a supportive spouse who set aside his career for hers, she might not have persisted in the academy. Again, department chairs and deans need to recognize that women have home responsibilities that male faculty generally do not have. This requires flexibility and other considerations when, for example, a childcare emergency becomes a priority over a department meeting.
- Tenure and promotion policies are generally dictated by the provost's office, requiring uniformity for all faculty. Thus, mentorship for a promotion and tenure plan is necessary from the first semester when a new STEM woman joins the

department. Though there are policies in place stipulating the benchmarks that must be met, it still behooves the department chair to accompany the faculty on the journey. Gender disparities that may derail successful promotion and tenure include inequitable teaching loads, advising overload, an excessive amount of service in the department, the college, and at the university level, gender and racial bias, insufficient time for scholarship, and a lack of mentorship. Our participants suggested that the tenure timeline be adjusted for women faculty who have babies and young children. It was further suggested that the pathway to reentering a tenure track position be more accessible for those who left to have and raise children.

- Engineering colleges need to note data from the Society of Women Engineers, as reported by Roy [21]. They indicate that the number of women in engineering in the USA has not increased in a generation, since the early 2000s. Among engineering faculty, recent statistics suggest that women of color represent less than 3% of full professors, about 6% of associate professors, and less than 9% of assistant professors [25].

Recommendations from Participants

One of the final interview questions invited participants to provide recommendations to graduate students, early-career professionals, deans, and department chairs. "Please share a few recommendations for women in graduate school," and "If you could share recommendations with STEM deans and chairs, what would they be?" The participants were forthcoming and offered recommendations that were consistent and pragmatic.

For Graduate Students

- One of the participants suggested: "Take every opportunity," stressing the importance of outside collaboration. "I would recommend they reach out to their networks, especially other women, more experienced women. And to develop those relationships early on."
- Outreach and seeking others, even if just for a cup of coffee to talk, was recommended with an important caveat: "Because you never know once you find those mutual interests, it may not be, you know, a grant solicitation that's next week, but maybe a year from now, you realize that."
- Another reason for networking may be helpful when you are looking for a new job. "So I'd encourage other women to network. And I shouldn't say limit it to women. But I've just found that's where I've gotten the most benefit with advocacy and straightforward information is from women."
- Virtual support networks were also encouraged. "And so I currently have, I think four right now, with people outside of my institution. So one of them is like a writing group where we share writing and then take turns providing feedback." Another group composed of women and men meets for accountability, to share goals and then report back 2 weeks later if the goals have been met. "Or these are

the challenges I faced. And when we-, we can ask questions of each other, like I have a challenge with this. Does anybody have any suggestions or recommendations?"

For Deans and Chairs

- Mentorship often came up with expectations that mentors, promised by a dean or chair, were expected and desirable. It was also recommended that it would be beneficial for department chairs and deans to have an individual one on one, maybe annually or even first semester, to kind of say, "this is all the support we're supposed to be providing. Are you receiving this? And if not, why." It was recommended to have this be a one-on-one conversation with one's chair, not a group process. "You don't want anybody, you know--, you don't want it to go back to your department chair that you're calling him or her out because they're not doing their job."

- One participant brought up the chilly climate "these other things that are happening for women and people of color--." "I think it would be helpful if deans and department chairs or administration would intentionally seek out those conversations to use self-assessment to understand how are we doing. Are we doing what we say we're going to do? And if not, what can be done?"

- In a particular college, the dean attempted to bring the women together through monthly lunches. Although there were good intentions, she observed that the sessions were not properly facilitated. In these large luncheons, women from the humanities, sciences, and other disciplines were brought together. The participant felt that she could not address social justice issues, as did her colleagues in the social sciences. With the chair and dean in the room, she observed that unfavorable comments she might make could affect her promotion and tenure process.

- One participant described her conversations with one of her mentors about being excluded and the experiences of microaggressions. The woman had been in the private sector and was surprised about the behavior in academic units. "I never felt like people were holding things against me because of my gender. I never had that impression." However, she had read about the chilly climate research and needed to make sense of what she was experiencing. This participant's recommendation was to do a reality check with someone trustworthy like a mentor. "And she kind of explained it to me like with the glass ceiling. The higher you get up, the more politics play a role. And so at lower levels, politics don't necessarily play a role. But as you move up through the system, that's where these microaggressions and these biases and these unhealthy workplaces start to play a bigger role." In short, the recommendation was to talk with someone else, a mentor, to gain insight into what one is experiencing.

Health and Mental Health in the Academy

Recent and historical reports about women in STEM have underscored the structures and systems in place that continue to undermine the success of women in STEM professions, as graduate students, faculty, and administrators. The National Academies of Sciences, Engineering, and Medicine published a Consensus Study Report [18] on the consequences of women's sexual harassment in the academic sciences, engineering, and medicine. The authors note that "the impact of sexual harassment extends across lines of industry, occupation, race, and social class." Their research demonstrates that sexual harassment negatively impacts an individual's physical and mental health and is associated with decreases in job satisfaction, organizational commitment, productivity, and performance.

Another study published in *JAMA Internal Medicine* (2018) reports that:

- Midlife women who had been victims of sexual assault were almost three times more likely to have significant depressive symptoms and two times more likely to suffer from anxiety than women who had not been sexually assaulted.
- Midlife women who had been sexually harassed were two times more likely to have an untreated high blood pressure than those who had been sexually harassed.
- Both categories of women were twice as likely to have trouble sleeping than those who had not been sexually harassed or assaulted [26].

These studies quantify what women have known for many years: that sexual harassment and assault can negatively affect mental and physical health and derail a promising career. Though these data are reported to higher education employers, the status quo prevails. Chapter 3 discussed the incidents of sexual harassment on college campuses that have been underreported and not investigated and the effects on women faculty. Being in male-dominated sciences and engineering puts women at risk, and the responsibility lies with university administrators, including deans and department chairs, to intervene when there is evidence of sexual harassment, bullying, and other oppressive behaviors impacting a woman's well-being.

STEM Diversity Initiatives and Resources

Diversity, equity, inclusion, and access (DEIA) initiatives are unfolding across university campuses. Although many focus on student enrollment and retention, particularly as this relates to students of color, more initiatives are prioritizing the recruitment, retention, and advancement of faculty, staff, and administrators from underrepresented groups, including STEM women. As a response to the racially motivated murder of George Floyd on May 25, 2020, in Minneapolis, and the many reported incidents of killings of Black men and women, protests across the country ensued in the midst of the COVID-19 pandemic, and there has been a heightened awareness of the need to focus on institutional DEIA initiatives for change. Examples of universities that are engaged in STEM diversity-related endeavors follow.

The University of Wisconsin has STEM diversity advocates who serve as role models and mentors and has a strong commitment to supporting a culture that values diversity and fosters inclusion in STEM. This program's mission is to provide mentorship, advice, and resources for the success of individuals in all STEM fields. This is an inclusive initiative that provides information, advice, and the mentorship necessary for the participant (student) success in all STEM fields. This program invited individuals to become part of a network of STEM advocates and mentors.

The Levy Library, Icahn School of Medicine at Mt. Sinai Hospital, New York City, provides a curated list of national organizations that address diversity in STEM. National organizations are listed for ethnic minority groups, persons with disabilities, LGBTQ individuals, students, and veterans. Associations, particularly for women, are included. For any university or STEM department seeking graduate students and faculty resources, these are "go-to" lists.

The Berkeley STEM Diversity Initiative is a wide-ranging network of 118 STEM diversity programs at the university or closely partnered with the campus. Among the objectives of the initiative are to (a) examine campus policies and practices that affect the goals of the initiative, (b) gather and analyze data about equity gaps and a campus climate that provide potential opportunities to partner with the university's Division of Equity and Inclusion, and (c) organize partnerships across the 118 STEM programs [23].

Partnerships are increasingly common for universities wanting to advance STEM diversity programs. In 2020, the University of Minnesota's College of Education and Human Development secured $26 million in NSF funding. Partners include the University of California at Berkeley, the University of California at Riverside, and Massachusetts General Hospital. Together, they aspire to create pathways for students, particularly undergraduates into STEM and then into the STEM workforce. The articulated values for this STEM diversity partnership are social justice, equity, diversity, and accessibility [16].

Recommendations for Psychologists

Coursework in the psychology of women is rarely required in clinical and counseling psychology training programs; yet, psychologists regularly work with women from all backgrounds and disciplines in psychotherapy. To our colleagues in graduate training programs and internship sites, we note that a single course in multicultural counseling or multicultural psychology with a chapter on women and other identity groups hardly prepares them to be feminist psychologists. Rossiter described a woman scientist who reportedly spent years in therapy because she was told she was "maladjusted." In her estimation, women try to "adjust" to an environment that does not value their contributions: "As scientists, they were typical women; as women, they were unusual scientists" [6]. It would not be surprising that the label of "maladjusted" has been applied to many women scientists by both men and women psychologists. Why? Because theories are men's formulations and dominant in contemporary textbooks. To this end, we recommend the following for psychology faculty, researchers, and clinicians:

- Prepare a reading list of prominent theories in the psychological development of women that can be introduced in required courses of life-span development, vocational psychology, multicultural psychology, advanced theories, clinical practice, and internship. These theories speak to women's socialization in a heteropatriarchal society and the harm it causes for self-regard and identity, among other consequences. As discussed in this book, the psychological development of women of color—African American, Asian American and Pacific Islander, American Indian, and Latinx—requires special attention. Knowledge about intersecting identities [3] and intersectionality [5] and the "othering" of diverse people in the USA are contextual considerations psychologists must consider in psychotherapy.
- Psychologists-in-training, and all psychologists, must engage in cultural competency development. This paradigm of awareness, knowledge, and skills is presented in the APA Guidelines on Education and Training, Research, Practice, and Organizational Change for Psychologists [1] and the Multicultural Counseling Competencies [24]. Cultural competency development is a lifelong process and begins with psychologists becoming aware of their gender and cultural identity values, biases, assumptions, and blinders that may cause them to be sexist, classist, and racist with women they see. A psychologist with unexamined gender-related biases may hold negative attitudes about women scientists that become barriers to the relationship and the issues the woman wants to address.
- Psychologists must become versed in Guidelines provided by the APA addressing different identity groups. Among these are APA Guidelines for Psychological Practice with Girls and Women [2]. This document presents strength-based guidelines and examples of how to affirm and engage girls and women. Guideline 4 states: *Psychologists are encouraged to use interventions and approaches with girls and women that are affirmative, developmentally appropriate, gender and culturally relevant, and effective* (p. 12). At no time should these guidelines be used in a formulaic way. Rather, psychology professors must guide graduate students to examine the sociopolitical context of institutions where women study and work so they can clarify with a client how the biases in these settings are causing self-doubts and adversity. Psychotherapy with a competent professional can be a positive experience for women scientists who find themselves in a chilly climate and second-guessing themselves because of harmful and non-supportive feedback.

- It is recommended that psychologists engaging in research with STEM women apply a qualitative research design that invites women to describe their hopes, challenges, and ways they thrive as scientists. Faculty teaching research design must also introduce feminist research methodology that recognizes women's marginality in STEM. Standpoint theory [10] and the APA Multicultural Guideline 6, Psychologists as Researchers emphasize the need to attend to the cultural context and positionality in research design, assessment, and interpretation of data [8].

Closing Thoughts

We embarked on our study and book project as the #metoomovement was taking center stage in the USA. Women from diverse backgrounds and occupations led national protests calling for attention to the exploitation of women. A psychologist, Dr. Christine Blasey Ford, spoke out against the appointment of a Supreme Court nominee, accusing him of sexually assaulting her in college. He was appointed just the same. In my (Arredondo) work with the Opportunities for UnderRepresented Scholars (OURS) Program, funded by NSF for 4 years, I gathered extensive anecdotal data through coaching the STEM women selected to participate in this program. I heard examples of how STEM women of color thrive amid oppressive, sexist academic units. Our book is built around a formal qualitative study we designed and conducted that substantiates what I (Arredondo) observed when coaching women of color. Although the participants in our study did not have smooth sailing and affirming work environments, they exhibited the emotional intelligence and stamina necessary to rise above the barriers of chilly climates, departmental cultures, and excessive work demands. Our participants are intelligent, well-grounded women who engage in perspective-taking, problem-solving, and awareness of the environment in which they find themselves. Although initially, some had challenges getting their careers underway, all have learned how to negotiate the labyrinth of the academy. It has been our privilege to bear witness to the stories of ten powerful women scientists.

References

1. American Psychological Association. (2003). Guidelines on multicultural education, training, research, practice, and organizational change for psychologists. *American Psychologist, 58*(5), 377–402. https://doi.org/10.1037/0003-066X.58.5.377.
2. American Psychological Association, Girls and Women's Guideline Group. (2018). *APA guidelines for psychological practice with girls and women* (Data set). American Psychological Association. https://doi.org/10.1037/e505882019-001.
3. Arredondo, P. (1996). *Successful diversity management initiatives: A blueprint for planning and implementation.* Thousand Oaks: Sage.

4. Arredondo, P. (2003). Resistance to multiculturalism in organizations. In J. S. Mio & G. Y. Iwamasa (Eds.), *Multicultural mental health research and resistance: Continuing challenges of the new millennium* (pp. 83–104). London: Brunner-Routledge.

5. Crenshaw, K. (1989). Demarginalizing the intersection of race and sex: A black feminist critique of antidiscrimination doctrine, feminist theory and antiracist politics. *University of Chicago Legal Forum, 1989*(1), 31.

6. Dominus, S. (2019, October). Women scientists were written out of history. It's Margaret Rossiter's lifelong mission to fix that. *Smithsonian Magazine.* https://www.smithsonianmag. com/science-nature/unheralded-women-scientists-finally-getting-their-due-180973082/

7. Eagly, A. H., & Karau, S. J. (2002). Role congruity theory of prejudice toward female leaders. *Psychological Review, 109*(3), 573. https://doi.org/10.1037/0033-295X.109.3.573.

8. Fouad, N. A., & Arredondo, P. (2007). *Becoming culturally oriented: Practical advice for psychologists and educators.* Washington, DC: American Psychological Association.

9. Hall, R. M., & Sandler, B. R. (1982). *The classroom climate: A chilly one for women?* https:// eric.ed.gov/?id=ED215628

10. Harding, S. G. (1986). *The science question in feminism.* Ithaca: Cornell University Press.

11. Henry, D. W. J., & Glenn, N. M. (2009). Black women employed in the ivory tower: Connecting for success. *Advancing Women in Leadership Journal, 29.* https://doi.org/10.18738/awl. v29i0.271.

12. Kramer, V. M., Konrad, A. M., & Erkut, S. (2006). *Critical mass on corporate boards: Why three or more women enhance governance.* Wellesley: Wellesley Centers for Women.

13. Lithwick, D. (2010, September 6). *The female factor: Will three women really change the supreme court? Newsweek.* https://www.newsweek.com/ can-three-women-really-change-supreme-court-71275

14. Miville, M. L. (2018). No rest for the nasty: Mentoring as mobilizing for change and advocacy. *The Counseling Psychologist, 46*(1), 100–115. https://doi.org/10.1177/0011000018754323.

15. Miville, M. L. (in press). Every Latina a potential leader: Advancing resistance capacities in higher education. *Journal of Hispanics in Higher Education.*

16. Moe, K. (2020, August 4). *NSF grant supports CEHD work toward diversity in STEM.* College of Education and Human Development. https://news.cehd.umn.edu/ nsf-grant-supports-cehd-work-toward-diversity-in-stem/

17. Muhs, G. G. Y, Niemann, Y. F., & González, C. G. (2012). *Presumed incompetent: The intersections of race and class for women in academia* (A. P. Harris, Ed.). University Press of Colorado.

18. National Academies of Sciences, Engineering, and Medicine, Policy and Global Affairs, Committee on Women in Science, Engineering, and Medicine, & Committee on the Impacts of Sexual Harassment in Academia. (2018). *Sexual harassment of women: Climate, culture, and consequences in academic sciences, engineering, and medicine* (F. F. Benya, S. E. Widnall, & P. A. Johnson, Eds.). National Academies Press (US). http://www.ncbi.nlm.nih.gov/books/ NBK507206/

19. Neville, H. A., Gallardo, M. E., & Sue, D. W. (2016). *The myth of racial color blindness: Manifestations, dynamics, and impact.* Washington, DC: American Psychological Association.

20. Niemann, Y. F., Muhs, G. G. y., & González, C. G. (2020). *Presumed incompetent II: Race, class, power, and resistance of women in academia.* Louisville: Utah State University Press.

21. Roy, J. (2019). *Engineering by numbers engineering statistics* (p. 40). American Society for Engineering Education. http://www.asee.org/documents/papers-and-publications/publications/college-profiles/2018-Engineering-by-Numbers-Engineering-Statistics-UPDATED-15-July-2019.pdf

22. Silbey, S. S. (2016, August 23). Why do so many women who study engineering leave the field? *Harvard Business Review.* https://hbr.org/2016/08/ why-do-so-many-women-who-study-engineering-leave-the-field

23. *STEM Equity and Inclusion Initiative|Diversity.* (2020). UC Berkeley, Division of Equity& Inclusion. https://diversity.berkeley.edu/initiatives/stem-equity-and-inclusion-initiative

24. Sue, D. W., Arredondo, P., & McDavis, R. J. (1992). Multicultural counseling competencies and standards: A call to the profession. *Journal of Multicultural Counseling and Development, 20*(2), 64–88. https://doi.org/10.1002/j.2161-1912.1992.tb00563.x.
25. *Survey of Doctoral Recipients.* (2015). National Science Foundation, National Center for Science and Engineering Statistics. https://ncsesdata.nsf.gov/doctoratework/2015/
26. Thurston, R. C., Chang, Y., Matthews, K. A., Känel, R. von, & Koenen, K. (2018). Association of sexual harassment and sexual assault with midlife women's mental and physical health. *JAMA Internal Medicine, 179*(1), 48–53. https://doi.org/10.1001/jamainternmed.2018.4886
27. Toosi, N. R., Mor, S., Semnani-Azad, Z., Phillips, K. W., & Amanatullah, E. T. (2019). Who CAN LEAN IN? The intersecting role of race and gender in negotiations. *Psychology of Women Quarterly, 43*(1), 7–21. https://doi.org/10.1177/0361684318800492.

Index

A
Academia, 83
Academia support
  career support, 73
  mentorship participants, 72
  peer support, 73
  sanity check, 73
  social support, 73
Academic culture
  campus culture, 46
  communication biases, 47
  context cultures, 47
  COVID-19 pandemic, 46
  institutional cultures, 47
  socialization, 47
  university culture, 46
  workplace, 47
Academic environments, 97
Academic identity, 69, 70
Academic self-worth, 69
Adverse identity self-perceptions
  imposter syndrome, 30, 31
  negative cognitive and emotional
    processes, 30
  self-esteem, 30
  stereotype threat, 31, 32
Affirmative Action, 57–58
Agentic leadership efficacy (ALE), 33
Alexandria Ocasio-Cortez (AOC), 87
Anima, 24
Anti-Latinx environment, 84
Assimilation, 52
Association for Women in Science (AWIS), 11
Attributions, 98

B
Black feminists, 20, 27
Bullying, 54

C
Campus culture, 46
Career decisions, 84, 85
Career development, women
  female-dominated professions, 8
  gender, 8
  physical characteristics, 8
  SCCT, 10
  STEM women, 9
  vocational psychology, 8
  women of color, 8, 9
Career function, 69, 70, 95
Career support, 73
Catalyst, 42
Chilly climates, 104
  academia, 57
  higher education, 48
    racism, 53
    sexism and ageism, 53
  imposter syndrome, 98
  unhealthy work environments, 77
  universities, 57
  women of color, 99
Civil Rights Act, 1964, 18
Communal behavior, 78
Communication biases, 47
Consumer goods businesses, 41
COVID-19, 29, 110
Cultural competency development, 50, 111

Cultural norms, 44
Culture
    institutions, 42
    organizations, 41, 42
    symbols, 41

D
Decision-making, 96
Dimensions of Identity model, 98
Dimensions of Personal Identity (DPI)
    interdependent identity, 28
    intersecting identities, 28, 30
    VERG, 29
    woman's life and career, 29
    women in STEM, 29
Dimensions of Personal Identity model, 51, 52
Diversity, equity, inclusion, and access
            (DEIA), 50, 96, 109
Double bind, women of color, 56

E
Economic and social well-being, 56
Emotional intelligence (EI), 33, 34
Equal Opportunity Commission (EOC), 57
Equal Pay Act, 1963, 18
Equality, 18
Excellence in Research (EiR) program, 57

F
Federally funded programs, 14
Feminism, 35
Feminist methodology, 63
Feminist multicultural psychology, 26
Feminist psychology
    black feminists, 20
    first-wave feminists, 17, 18
    neuroses, 21
    origins, 21
    Psychology of Women (*see* Psychology
        of Women)
    second-wave feminism, 18, 19
    self-enhancement/self-employment, 21
    socialization, 21
    sociocultural and environmental
            contexts, 21
    third-wave feminism, 19, 20
    women, 17
Financial institution, 42
First-wave feminists, 17, 18
Free communication, 80, 81

G
Gatekeepers, 46
Gender, 20, 53, 98
Gender-based barriers, 91
Gender-based hostility, 92
Gender-based structural barriers, 97
Gender discrimination, 42
Glass ceiling, 42, 44, 49

H
Healthy environments
    expectations, 79
    recommendations, 80
        free communication, 80, 81
        open communication, 80, 81
        support groups, 80
        transparent norms, 79
Heterosexism, 46
Higher education
    assimilation, 52
    chilly climate, 48
    double bind, women of color, 56
    evidence-based voices, 52
    Hofstede's index, 49
    lawsuits, 58
    persons of color, 50
    positionality, 52
    racism, 53
    sciences, 57
    sex discrimination, 53
    sexism and ageism, 53
    sexual harassment, 54–56
    sexual misconduct, 54, 55
    university culture, 46
Hiring process, 105
Historically black college/university
            (HBCU), 34, 83
History of women scientists
    American Men in Science (book), 7
    Hidden Figures, 6
    hierarchical segregation, 4
    Latinas in STEM, 6, 7
    Maria Mitchell, 4
    Matilda effect, 4
    pioneers in STEM, 4, 5
    public spaces, 7
    restrictive logic, 4
    territorial segregation, 4
    the Lancet, 7
Hostile environments, 88, 89
Hostile work environment, 100
Human computers, 6

I

Imposter syndrome, 30, 31, 52, 96–98
Inequities, 42
Intersecting identities, 21, 27, 35, 52
Intersectionality, 20, 22, 25

L

Latinas in STEM, 6, 7
Leadership
    ALE, 33
    attention, 33
    emotional intelligence, 33, 34
    gender role, 33
    higher education, 32
    men's socialization, 32
    mujerista, 33
    relational-cultural theory, 32
    resonant leadership, 34
    role congruity theory, 33
    women-centered research, 32

M

Masculinity, 49
Matilda effect, 4
Mentorship
    academic environments, 70
    career advancement, 95
    career function, 69, 70, 95
    functions, 69
    imposter syndrome, 96
    lack of support, 72
    participants, 96
    professional growth, 69
    psychosocial functions, 70, 95
    resonant leadership, 96
    self-esteem, 70
    STEM, 71, 72
    tenure process, 70
    undergraduate research, 70
    woman-to-woman mentoring
        relationships, 96
Microaggressions, 77, 92, 93, 98, 104, 108
Microcultures, 41
Microinequities, 48
Multicultural counseling competency (MCC),
        33, 34, 50
Multicultural organizational development
    assimilation, 52
    chilly climate, 53
    cultural competency development, 50
    DEI, 51

DEIA, 50
Dimensions of Personal Identity
        model, 51, 52
    diversity, 50
    ethnic/racial group identity, 53
    gender, 52
    higher education, 50, 52
    imposter syndrome, 52
    intersectional invisibility, 53
    MCC, 50
    sense of agency, 53
    social psychology, 51
    systemic barriers, 51
    systemic sexism and racism, 51
    T3 professionals, 51
    twenty-first century, 51
    unconscious bias, 50
    white male privilege, 52
    women of color, 53

N

National Academy, 10
National Academy of Engineering, 10
National Academy of Sciences (NAS), 10
National Science Foundation, 57
Neuroses, 21
NSF Broadening Participation Initiative, 57

O

Office of Civil Rights (OCR), 11
Open communication, 80, 81, 97
Opportunities for UnderRepresented Scholars
        (OURS) Program, 112
Organizational culture, 41
    anti-discrimination laws, workplaces, 49
    cultural dimensions, 49
    Hofstede's index, higher education, 49, 50
    masculinity, 49
    multicultural organizational development
        (*see* Multicultural organizational
        development)
    universities, 49
Organizations, 43, 44

P

Parental leave, 74
Peer support, 96
Personal quality, 83, 84
Power and privilege, 98
Presumed Incompetent (Book), 52, 53, 104

Principal investigators (PI), 92
Promotion and tenure (P&T) processes, 98
Psychic imprints, 23
Psychologists, 112
Psychology of women
    anima, 24
    APA, 111
    children's education, 23
    clinical and counseling psychology
            training programs, 110
    courses, 111
    cultural and gender identity, 23
    cultural competency development, 111
    feminine development theory, 24
    feminist movement, 23
    feminist organizations, 22
    Feminist Theory (journal), 22
    intersectionality, 22
    psychic imprints, 23
    psychological development, 22
    psychotherapy, 111
    science, 22
    social and cultural contexts, 22
    standpoint theory, 26, 27
    women of color, 25, 26
    women's cognitive processes, 25
Psychosocial functions, 69, 70
Psychotherapy, 110, 111

R
Race and ethnicity, 98
Racial and gender stereotypes, 98
Resistance, 105
Resonant leadership, 34, 96
Restrictive logic, 4
Role congruity theory, 33
Role theory, 45

S
Salary inequity, 44
Sciences, 57
Second-wave feminism, 18, 19
Self-advocacy, 100
    career decisions, 84, 85
    chilly climates, 99
    gender role, 99
    mentoring approach, 99
    personal quality, 83, 84, 99
    seeking support, 85, 86
    sense of agency, 99
    women of color, 99
Self-concept, 92

Self-conception, 25
Self-determination, 17
Self-efficacy, 9, 30, 33, 53
Self-esteem, 70
Self-perceptions, 101
Self-respect, 99
Sense of agency, 53, 99
Sexed-based category, 27
Sexism, 105
Sexual assault, 109
Sexual harassment, 109
    academy, 54
    higher education, 54
    reasons, 54
    sciences, 55, 56
Sexual misconduct, 54, 55
Sexual orientation, 9
Sexual politics (1970), 18
Social advocacy, 105
Social cognitive career theory (SCCT), 10
Social norms, 44
Social psychology, 51
Social role theory, 78
Social sciences, 54
Social support, 73
Socialization, 35, 49
Societal influences, 9
Society of Women Engineers (SWE), 10, 107
Sojourner Truth, 18
Space race, 6
Standpoint theory, 27, 63, 98, 112
STEM academic settings
    study limitation, 100
    women's experiences, 100
STEM academies and federally funded
            program, women, 13, 14
STEM diversity programs, 110
STEM pipeline
    academy, 13
    agricultural sciences, 11
    doctoral-level scientists and engineers, 13
    engineering faculty, 13
    ethnicity and race, 12
    gender, 13
    health and medical sciences, 11
    life sciences-related discipline, 12
    race and ethnicity, 13
    Society of Women Engineers, 12
STEM women, 9, 58
    career advancement, 104
    chilly climates, 104, 112
    climate, 103
    critical mass, 105
    culture, 103

deans and chairs, 104
DEIA, 109, 110
demographic change, 104
diversity initiatives, 109, 110
engineering students, 103
governance, 105
health and mental health,
        academy, 109
internship experience, 103
leadership, 104
Matilda effect, 103
microaggressions, 104
National organizations, 110
partnerships, 110
policies, 105–107
Presumed Incompetent (book), 104
psychologists, 112
recommendations
        deans and chairs, 108
        graduate students, 107
resistance, 105
retention, 104
sexism, 103, 105
systemic racism, 104–105
unconscious bias, 105
unhealthy environment, 105
women of color, 112
STEM Women of Color Conclave
        (SWOCC), 11
Structural barriers, academia
    AOC, 87
    gender-based barriers, 91
    hiring processes, 90
    hostile environments, 87, 89
    masculine forms, 89
    microaggressions, 92
    negative experience, 88
    negative psychological impact, 92
    patriarchal attitudes and behaviors, 88
    principal investigators, 92
    self-advocacy strategies, 89
    STEM disciplines, 89
    tenure process, 91
    toxic behaviors, 92
    toxic environment, 91
    women in STEM, 88
    women, workplace, 87
Superwoman syndrome, 45
Support groups, 80, 97
Support systems
    academia support, 72, 73
    mentorship (*see* Mentorship)
    personal decision-making, 95
    work/life balance, 73–75

T
Tending and befriending, 45
Tenure and promotion policies, 106
Thematic analysis
        academic STEM environments, 63
        coding process, 66
        demographic questions, 64
        feminist methodology, 63
        interview data, 64
        participant demographics, 66
        participants, 65
        procedure, 64
        qualitative method, 65
        questionnaire protocol, 64
        semi-structured interview protocol, 65
        subjective experiences, 63
        thematic map, 67
        theoretical approach, 65
Thematic coding, 66
Thematic map, 67
Theoretical approach, 65
Third-wave feminism, 19, 20
Toxic environment, 91
Train-the-trainer (T3) program, 51

U
Unhealthy work environments
        chilly climate, 77
        defaulted roles, 78
        feedback, 77
        themes, 77
        transparency, 77
        unshared workload, 79
University culture, 46
Unshared workload, 79
Unsupportive environments, 96

V
Virtual support networks, 107
Visible Ethnic Racial Groups (VERG), 29
Vocational psychology, 8

W
White feminist, 19
Women in STEM, 31, 63
Women in the World of Work, 2021
        administrative leadership, 45
        DEI initiatives, 45
        feminist, 44
        labor fields, 44
        medicine, 44

Women in the World of Work (*cont.*)
   role theory, 45
   salary inequity, 44
   science professions, 44
   social norms, 44
   social roles experience, 45
   stress response, 45
   superwoman syndrome, 45
   workforce, 44
Women of color, 1, 8, 9, 25, 26, 52,
      97–99, 104
Women scientists
   Marie Curie, 1
   professional associations, 10, 11
   STEM professions, 1
   women of color, 1
Women's liberation movement, 19

Women's rights legislation, USA
   affects, 2, 3
   students, higher education, 2
Women's ways of knowing, 96
Work environments, 96, 97
Work/life balance, 73, 106
Workplaces
   Cult of Domesticity, 43
   diversity, 57, 58
   gender role, 43
   hospital settings, 43
   inclusion, 57, 58
   organizations, 44
   stratification, 44
   womanhood, 43
   women in organizations, 43
   women professionals, 44